T0009589

Spirits, Beers & Séances

About the Author

Steele Alexandra Douris is an author, artist, and Victorianist, specializing in Victorian spiritualism, crime fiction, and the gothic. She is a PhD candidate in the English department at Stanford University, where she has taught courses on nineteenth-century spiritualism and ghost stories. She holds an MA in English from Stanford University and a BA in anthropology from the University of Texas at Austin. When she's not hunting down obscure Victorian texts, she writes fiction and enjoys fantasy illustration and worldbuilding. Steele splits her time between Texas and California, towing her mountain of sketchbooks and journals with her wherever she goes.

STEELE ALEXANDRA DOURIS

Spirits Seers & Séances

VICTORIAN SPIRITUALISM, MAGIC & THE SUPERNATURAL

Llewellyn Publications | Woodbury, Minnesota

FIRST EDITION
First Printing, 2023

Book design by Christine Ha
Cover design by Shannon McKuhen

Photography is used for illustrative purposes only. The persons depicted may not endorse or represent the book's subject.

Llewellyn Publications is a registered trademark of Llewellyn Worldwide Ltd.

Library of Congress Cataloging-in-Publication Data (Pending)
ISBN: 978-0-7387-7461-9

Llewellyn Publications
A Division of Llewellyn Worldwide Ltd.
2143 Wooddale Drive
Woodbury, MN 55125-2989
www.llewellyn.com

Printed in the United States of America

To my mother,
my first and best friend.

Contents

Contents

Exercises

Exercises

Introduction
An Invitation to the Night-Side

A woman wearing a black veil convenes a séance. A girl hears a mysterious rapping from the back of her wardrobe and reveals to her parents that she is communicating with the spirit of a murder victim. A magician puts a volunteer from the audience into a trance. A fortune-teller hunches over a crystal ball, offering insight and warnings to the girls who have lined up to ask about their future husbands.

Everyone knows what Victorian magic *looks* like. In fact, in our modern moment, so deeply infused with nostalgia and so culturally obsessed with witches, much of the imagery, language, and practice deemed "magical" or "witchy" is borrowed from the Victorians. It's hard to move in many modern occult circles without tripping over the Victorians. And yet, somehow, in the process of becoming ubiquitous, the Victorians have also become invisible.

The autumn before I began work on this book, I taught a college course focused on the connection between nineteenth-century ghost stories and Victorian practices of spiritualism and mediumship. One day in class, a student commented on the striking modernity of many of the spiritualist techniques and practices we were studying. Most of them, she pointed out, are still in practice in some modified form today. Her observation was correct; and yet, despite the omnipresence of Victorian-tinged magic, there is often little understanding of the spiritual, cultural, and historical foundations of Victorian spiritualism.

Who were the Victorians? What made them turn to séances or automatic writing or crystal balls? What were they afraid of? What did they want? Whom were they searching for? Like an organ taken from a body, Victorian spiritualist practices are severed from their cultural context and from the vital systems that surrounded them in their own day. My goal in writing this book is to explore that vital context.

Looking Deeper

We are living in an age of aesthetics. Whatever your aesthetic of choice, there's likely to be hundreds (to thousands) of dedicated Instagram accounts, a slew of Pinterest boards, and a plethora of TikToks. If your tastes lean toward the spooky, witchy, or gothic, then you've probably seen your fair share of Victorian-inspired aesthetics: Victorian mansions and Victorian nightgowns; corsets and candelabras; antique armchairs and first editions of Dracula … the list could go on and on. Sometimes, it seems as though anything that looks about one hundred to two years old is automatically labeled "spooky" or "witchy," regardless of whether it was seen as such in its own time. But if everything that even looks Victorian becomes "witchy," then it's hard to know what the Victorians themselves would have considered magical or otherworldly. They looked at life with very different lenses, though they were just as fixated with the supernatural and occult as we are now. The aim of this book is to look beyond the aesthetics of Victorian magic and examine the theories and practices at its heart. Exactly what techniques were the Victorians using in their magic? How did they think, write, and speak about spiritualism? What were their philosophies, beliefs, fears, and curiosities?

Introduction

The Victorian era was a marriage of knowledge and superstition; invention and intuition; discovery and tradition; and technology and myth. Many Victorians saw no clear delineation between science and spiritualism, and most Victorian spiritualists were quick to adopt the very latest technologies in their quest to hone their psychic powers. As early photography took off in the nineteenth century, spiritualists quickly used the new medium to try to capture evidence of ghosts and spirits. At the same time, the Pre-Raphaelite painters were having their heyday, trying to reach backward through the mists of time to tap into what they saw as an earlier, truer source of artistic power. Vivid images of the ancient, feminine divine filled their canvases as they painted the women of Greek epics, Roman mythology, Arthurian legend, and Shakespearean theater.

Much like us, the Victorians were constantly struggling with their own relationship to the technologies that surrounded them. They were fascinated by the latest scientific advances but deeply nostalgic for the days of yore. They loved their telegrams, photographs, and phonographs, but they were also deeply ambivalent about their own brave new world. As the world became increasingly industrialized and urbanized, the Victorians looked for safety, comfort, and enchantment in their own homes. This is the era that spawned a thousand fantasies of the cozy domestic: families clustered around a roaring fire, fathers reading to their children by candlelight, mothers tucking their little ones into bed on stormy nights. But this is also the era that gave us some of the most hair-raising Gothic tales of all time. The Victorians loved ghost stories, and the genre was intensely popular in the nineteenth century. To the Victorians, homes were sites of both cozy domesticity and chilling horror.

The Victorians had a keen sense of both the light and the shadow of the domestic. Like many people today, the Victorians felt a profound urge to retreat into personal spiritual and creative practice to shield themselves from the public sphere. Though it may sound quaint today, the city centers of the nineteenth century felt bustling, overwhelming, rife with social problems, and deeply unsettling to the Victorians, as industrialization was still a newer and relatively uncomfortable phenomenon. Like us, they yearned to turn inward, to close out the dizzying rush of technological advances and political developments, and find a calm, grounded center. While we worry over the corrupting influence of social media and the 24/7 news cycle, the Victorians were alarmed by the explosion of sensationalized newspaper reporting and the penny press.

Like the Victorian era itself, this book is a blending of old and new, of technological and intuitive, of spiritual and scientific. The title of this introduction takes inspiration from a nineteenth-century catalog of supernatural phenomena. In 1848, Catherine Crowe, a Victorian novelist turned paranormal researcher, published *The Night-Side of Nature, or, Ghosts and Ghost-Seers*. *The Night-Side of Nature* is Crowe's exhaustive catalog of an array of supernatural manifestations. Almost two hundred years later, inspired by Crowe, I've taken on this project to introduce readers to the richness and variety of Victorian spiritualist beliefs and practices.

How to Approach This Book

Given the depth and complexity of Victorian spiritualism, all the chapters in this book could easily be books themselves. However, the point of this work is to explore the many flavors of spiritualism and the supernatural as they manifested across the nineteenth century, so I have tried to quickly get to the heart and philosophy of each practice, offer examples of popular techniques, and design exercises that allow readers to practice Victorian methods—or explore nineteenth-century mindsets.

The Try It Yourself exercises at the end of each chapter are intended to foster personal growth and experimentation while helping readers connect to the beliefs and values that were at the core of the Victorian spiritualist movement. Whether you undertake the experiments as seriously as the most reverent Victorian or try them for some Hallowe'en fun with friends, I hope that they will provide opportunities for reflection and learning.

Remember, the Victorian era was when writers such as H. G. Wells and Jules Verne walked in the footsteps of Mary Shelley and kicked the newborn science fiction genre into high gear, so feel free to mix up your own unique blend of the old and the new. The Victorians loved speculating about new and upcoming technology, so, if you can think of exciting ways to update the techniques in this book using your devices of choice, do it! That is a deeply Victorian impulse.

The Origin of This Book

Literature and archaeology have long been two sources of fascination for me. After studying anthropology and archaeology as an undergraduate, I decided to switch gears for graduate school. I enrolled in a literature PhD program and eventually found myself researching Victorian ghosts. I studied the roots of the Victorian gothic, the rise of Victorian spiritualism, and the very first paranormal investigations. *Spirits, Seers, and Séances* draws upon years of research into Victorian customs, spirituality, and superstition. In writing this book, I have relied on my background in anthropology and literary history, as well as my experience teaching students about Victorian spiritualism.

As a graduate student at Stanford University researching Victorian literature and spiritualism, the past has often felt close enough to touch. The university was founded by grieving parents, Leland

and Jane Stanford, who established the school in honor of their dead son, Leland Junior. The Stanfords themselves both attended séances, and they are buried on the university grounds in a forbidding mausoleum guarded by sphinxes.[1] The Winchester Mystery House, an eerie Victorian mansion turned haunted museum (recently the subject of a supernatural horror film), is just a short drive away. All of this is to say: the Victorians are everywhere. We stand on their roads, on their foundations, on their bones. We assign their books, admire their art, and resurrect them repeatedly in our period dramas and historical fiction. We grapple with many of the same anxieties and inhibitions, however much we deny it … And we love their magic.

Who Were the Victorians?

No really, who were the Victorians? When people talk about the Victorians, there are a few definitions they might be using. The narrowest definition of *the Victorians* refers to people who lived under the rule of Queen Victoria, who was ruler of the United Kingdom of Great Britain and Ireland from 1837 to 1901. The United States, obviously, was not ruled by Queen Victoria. However, there was a lot of cultural overlap between the United Kingdom and the United States during that period, and so many scholars recognize a kind of transatlantic cultural Victorianism that includes the residents of the United States as American Victorians in a cultural, rather than political, sense. When I refer to Victorians in this book, I will be using the term in that relatively loose sense: to refer to North American, Irish, and British people who lived between 1837 and 1901.

The period that preceded the Victorian era in Britain is known as the Georgian era, and it lasted from 1714 to 1837. Coming in at

....

1. Johnston, "Mrs. Stanford and the Netherworld," *Stanford Magazine*.

the tail end of the Georgian era was a subperiod known as the Regency era, which is the period that gave us empire silhouette dresses and Jane Austen. That's right—neither Jane Austen nor her books were Victorian; Austen died almost twenty years before Victoria took the throne. Though the Victorians are now almost infamous for their repression and restraint, there was more to them than just their inhibitions; an undercurrent of sensationalism, melodrama, and mysticism ran through their literature, art, and popular culture.

A Word of Caution

The Victorian era was also a time of extraordinary cruelty. Every -ism imaginable, from ableism and classism to racism and sexism, was in full swing, and much of the new science being done during the nineteenth century reinforced oppressive and violent power structures. Psychology and psychiatry were weaponized against women, the poor, people of color, and those with disabilities. The British Empire had swallowed land all over the world, and its rule was brutally cruel and extractive. In the United States, slavery was legal for almost half of the Victoria era.

It is possible to like or even love certain aspects of a bygone era while also denouncing others; as a Victorianist, I know this well. Honesty is key; acknowledging the reality of the horror and cruelty is imperative. Admitting the truth does not have to mean abandoning the era entirely. If it did, then we would also have to abandon our own era because the present moment is also rife with violence, oppression, imperialism, and terror. Honesty and openness about the many failings of the Victorians can lend depth and wisdom to our understanding of their era and ours.

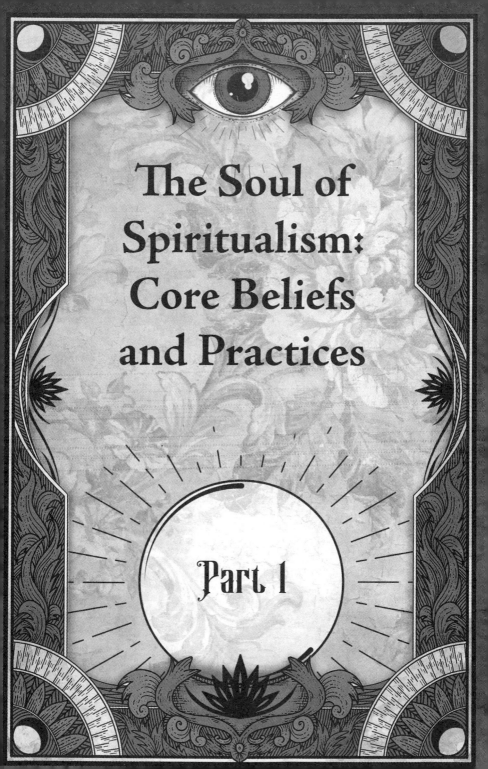

The Soul of Spiritualism: Core Beliefs and Practices

Part 1

Chapter 1
Séances and Spirit Communication: The Heart of Spiritualism

Shortly after we had said The Lord's Prayer, we saw some glimmering lights, and then a lovely sparkling one, which rose up spirally until it was just above the level of our heads, where it gradually faded away. We then heard the spirits making a great commotion among the things on the table, and throwing the tubes, sheets of paper, &c., on the ground...

—GEORGIANA HOUGHTON,
EVENINGS AT HOME IN SPIRITUAL SÉANCE[2]

If Victorian visions of spirits and the supernatural have outlived the nineteenth century and shaped our modern understanding of the paranormal, then the most powerful example of spiritualism's endurance is the séance. While there have likely been forms and practices of spirit communication for as long as the earth has held humans, the séance, or spirit circle, is a specific flavor of spirit communication bequeathed to us by the Victorians.[3] It has seeped into many aspects of our culture and many genres of our media.

....
2. Houghton, *Evenings at Home in Spiritual Séance*, 32.
3. Seeman, *Speaking with the Dead in Early America*, 266.

Paranormal investigators use séances in their work. Many modern witches, Neopagans, and occult practitioners incorporate séances into their personal practices. And, of course, the séance has long been a staple of the supernatural horror genre; books, films, and television abound with terrifying tales of corrupted spirit communication and séances gone wrong.

The Rise of Spiritualism

The story of spiritualism begins, as so many stories do, with a family moving into an eerie old house. When John and Margaret Fox relocated their family to Hydesville, New York, the farmhouse they moved into already had an unsettling reputation; some of the previous occupants had been frightened by mysterious rapping sounds at night. The Fox family moved into the house in 1847, and by early 1848, they reported hearing the noises themselves; at night, the farmhouse echoed with odd knocks and enigmatic raps of no discernible origin. The noises were said to be particularly alarming to the two youngest Fox girls, Margaretta (aged 14) and Catherine (aged 11).[4] In March of 1848, matters came to a head, as was later, rather dramatically, recounted by Sir Arthur Conan Doyle in his two-volume *History of Spiritualism*:

> *Finally, upon the night of March 31 there was a very loud and continued outbreak of inexplicable sounds. It was on this night that one of the great points of psychic evolution was reached, for it was then that young Kate Fox challenged the unseen power to repeat the snaps of her fingers. That rude room, with its earnest, expectant, half-clad occupants with eager upturned faces, its circle of candlelight, and its heavy*

....
4. Doyle, *The History of Spiritualism*, vol. 1, 57–58.

shadows lurking in the corners, might well be made the subject of a great historical painting ... The child's challenge, though given with flippant words, was instantly answered. Every snap was echoed by a knock.[5]

Mrs. Fox was stunned by the apparent communication between her younger daughter and some invisible force, and she began asking the spirit questions. When she asked the spirit how many children she'd borne, the spirit knocked seven times, which was the correct answer.

As Margaretta and Catherine continued to communicate with the spirit, neighbors came over to witness the phenomenon. The spirit was asked a series of yes or no questions about its identity and origins with shocking results; it claimed to be the ghost of a murdered peddler who had been buried in the cellar. Naturally, this caused something of a stir in the neighborhood. Neighbors were questioned about any local peddlers who might have gone missing several years before, and the cellar of the Fox farmhouse was partially excavated in search of the peddler's body.[6] The search for the murdered peddler ultimately stretched on for years; the investigation at the Fox farmhouse is discussed further in chapter 5.

However, while the case of the peddler's ghost was to remain unresolved for decades, news of the Hydesville Rappings spread rapidly. Catherine and Margaretta found themselves at the center of intense public interest, and they eventually began holding sessions professionally. Their work sparked an international spirit communication craze, and the young Fox sisters went on to become two of the most famous mediums of all time.

....

5. Doyle, *The History of Spiritualism*, vol. 1, 59.
6. Doyle, *The History of Spiritualism*, vol. 1, 60–66.

After Margaretta and Catherine paved the way, the practice of sitting together in groups to seek communion with the spirit-realm became a common pastime, a powerful healing tool for the bereaved, and even a viable profession. These sittings became commonly known as séances (*séance* comes from the French word for *session*), but Victorians also often used the terms *spirit circle* or *sitting* interchangeably with *séance*. People who engaged in regular spirit communication became known as spiritualists, and the practice of spiritualism rapidly spread across the United States and throughout the United Kingdom and Europe.

The budding spiritualist movement merged with the existing practice of mesmerism, or animal magnetism, which is detailed in chapter 2. Spiritualist mediums combined mesmerism and spiritualism by entering the trance state during séances to allow spirits to speak through them verbally. While some séances were small, private affairs led by a single medium for a small group, many spiritualists began giving trance lectures. During these lectures, the medium would enter a trance and allow the spirits to speak at length through them about various topics. Trance lectures were often very public, and crowds would pack in to see possessed mediums give speeches about life after death, talk about the experience of being a disembodied spirit, or even offer a spirit's perspective on current events.[7]

Spiritualism also gave rise to several important occultist and paranormal groups. The popularity of spiritualism was instrumental in the rise of Theosophy, which began with the founding of the Theosophical Society in New York City in 1875. Theosophy and spiritualism shared an abiding interest in the supernatural, but they were separate movements with different aims. Spiritualism was focused on making spirit communication accessible to all; the

....

7. Lehman, *Victorian Women and the Theatre of Trance*, 79.

spiritualists' goal was for anyone to be able to commune with the spirits of the dead. Theosophy, on the other hand, was oriented toward the pursuit of mystical secrets and the development of occult powers; it was much more dogmatic and structured with a clear hierarchy.[8] While spiritualism and Theosophy were separate movements, there was a lot of overlap in their practices and communities throughout the nineteenth century. Another important occult group with strong ties to spiritualism was the Hermetic Order of the Golden Dawn, which was founded in Britain in 1887. The Golden Dawn was a relatively short-lived society, but it had an outsized influence on Western occultism, and it helped give rise to modern Wicca.

The popularity of spiritualism grew for decades and then seemed to waver around the turn of the century as a series of demoralizing scandals and a few high-profile debunkings rocked the spiritualist community and tarnished its reputation. However, spiritualism experienced a rapid resurgence in the 1920s after World War I decimated a generation, leaving countless mourners seeking contact with their lost loved ones.[9] After that final surge, spiritualism's popularity began to fade in earnest. While spiritualism still exists and is practiced today, it no longer has the prominence that it once did.

The Politics and Culture of Spiritualism

So, why were the United States and the United Kingdom so receptive to spiritualism and its teachings during the Victorian era? Part of the allure of spiritualism was its flexibility; it wasn't overwhelmingly dogmatic, and it could be combined with all kinds of

....

8. Braude, *Radical Spirits*, 178.
9. Oppenheim, *The Other World*, 2.

existing religious and political beliefs.[10] The core tenet of Victorian spiritualism was that spirits existed and communication with them was possible. Beyond that, there was quite a bit of variation in the beliefs and philosophies of individual practitioners. Though mainstream Christian establishments tended to reject spiritualism, there were plenty of devout Christian spiritualists who saw their work at the séance table as part and parcel of their Christianity.[11]

In modern tales of the supernatural, séances often serve sinister purposes; they are the open door that lets the monsters in. For the Victorians, however, the séance was not supposed to be a frightening experience. To many spiritualists, the spirit circle was either a religious experience, a scientific experiment, or some combination of the two. As a result, Victorians were more likely to enter the circle with an attitude of reverence or curiosity than fear. Many practitioners wanted spiritualism recognized as a legitimate scientific field, and they saw themselves as scientific investigators working on the cutting edge of modern inquiry. However, mainstream Victorian scientists grew increasingly hostile toward spiritualism as the nineteenth century progressed. Some of the scientific establishment's animosity toward spiritualism stemmed from skepticism, but some of it was based on more personal prejudices. Scientific fields during the Victorian era were quite hostile to women, the poor, and anyone else "othered" by the nineteenth century's rigid social system. Spiritualism was comparatively more accepting of women, people of color, and others who found the doors of academic science closed to them.[12] Spiritualism's more tolerant attitude led to more diversity in

....

10. Oppenheim, *The Other World*, 82.
11. Oppenheim, *The Other World*, 67.
12. Vanessa D. Dickerson, *Victorian Ghosts in the Noontide*, 44–45.

its ranks, but that diversity also made spiritualism even less likely to be recognized as legitimate by more exclusionary fields.

The spiritualist outlook also appealed to the dreamers and idealists of the nineteenth century. Spiritualism was a deeply optimistic movement. Many Victorian spiritualists spoke of the rise of spiritualism as a crucial inflection point in human history; they hoped that they were ushering in a new age of widespread spirit communication.[13] They envisioned a new era during which the bereaved could stay in regular contact with their beloved dead until their own deaths. Spiritualists framed death as the passage into what they called spirit-life, and they spoke of the "spirit-land" or the "border-land"—a place where spirits congregated and could be communicated with. The goal of spiritualism was to see a time when the death of a loved one didn't feel like a death at all, but more like having a loved one move to a faraway place (from which they could only communicate by automatic writing or channeled trance speech). This vision of a new, griefless era was deeply comforting to lots of people, especially the bereaved.

Spiritualism was the hybrid child of religious fervor, scientific curiosity, and nineteenth-century mysticism, but it was also born of grief. Many spiritualists first experimented with spirit communication out of a desire to contact a lost loved one. They attended séances not to learn more about the spirit-world, but to grapple with unbearable loss. For grieving Victorians, visits to mediums or spirit circles were often part of the healing process. They could say whatever had been left unsaid, receive assurances that their loved ones were watching over them, and resurrect relationships that had been tragically sundered. This link between spiritualism and grief is evidenced by the way spiritualism surged in the United States after the

....
13. Lehman, *Victorian Women and the Theatre of Trance*, 83–84.

mass casualties of the American Civil War[14] and then peaked again after the combined assault of the Spanish Flu and World War I, both of which resulted in the premature deaths of tens of millions.[15]

Spiritualism was also closely linked to many progressive policies and platforms. As spiritualism first took off in America, it was championed by members of the "radical" Quaker community, which linked it to the abolition of slavery, women's rights, and pacifism. The ties between spiritualism and the women's rights movement were particularly strong. Many of the most popular mediums were women, and professional mediumship gave Victorian women a chance to strike out and earn a living on their own terms and under their own name.[16] Given spiritualism's progressive bent, it might be tempting to think of the spiritualists as morally righteous crusaders who were always on the right side of history, but it's important to retain the nuance of the incredibly wide range of spiritualist beliefs. It would be easy to paint the entire movement with a broad brush, but the reality is that while many spiritualists were trying to do good work, bigotry, racism, and misogyny still existed within the spiritualist community.

The Spirits of the Circle

To the spiritualists, psychic ability was something in between an innate gift and a finely honed skill. They did believe that certain people were innately more psychically gifted than others, but they also believed that almost anyone could work to improve their capacity for clairvoyance and spirit communication. Encouraging amateur investigators in their psychical experiments was an important part of spiritualist culture. People were encouraged to attend large

....

14. Seeman, *Speaking with the Dead in Early America*, 268–69.
15. Oppenheim, *The Other World*, 2.
16. Lehman, *Victorian Women and the Theatre of Trance*, 81–85.

spiritualist trance lectures and other events, but they were also encouraged to experiment with small spirit circles at home.[17]

One feature most experienced mediums had in common was a long-standing relationship with specific benign, protective spirits. These benevolent spirits were usually referred to as "spirit guides," but they were also called "spirit controls" because of their ability to take control of the medium's body during sessions of trace speaking, automatic writing, or other forms of channeled communication. These guides were often the spirit of a deceased individual who had once been close to the medium, but they could also be a random spirit who had made themselves known to the medium over a series of sessions. Most Victorian mediums had at least one or two core spirit controls, and some had quite a few.[18]

The protective powers of Victorian spirit guides tended to be limited to the shadowy realm of the spirits. When it came to earthly matters, these spirits could usually only offer wisdom, advice, or warnings; they weren't usually credited with the ability to intervene in and alter the course of human events on earth. However, in the spirit-world, spirit guides were thought to have quite a bit of protective potency, especially when it came to defending their medium of choice. One important role of a Victorian spirit guide was to protect the medium from being possessed by a malicious spirit or by too many spirits; the spirit guide could block other spirits from entering and speaking through their medium. In this way, the guide acted like a safety valve in the other realm, ensuring that the medium didn't become overwhelmed or possessed by malignant or mischievous entities.

....

17. Braude, *Radical Spirits*, 19–25.
18. See Lehman, *Victorian Women and the Theatre of Trance*, 122, 127–29 for an account of Victorian medium Cora Richmond's varied spirit controls.

Benevolent spirits were the focus of spiritualist activities, but spiritualism did recognize the existence of malevolent spirits. While prominent spiritualists argued that the benefits of spirit communication outweighed the risks, they advocated for what they saw as a commonsense attitude toward dangers from beyond the veil. Professional mediums tended to emphasize that beginners couldn't know for sure which spirit they were *really* channeling—not at first—and so a healthy degree of skepticism was important. If the spirit claimed to be a certain person, especially someone that the medium had known in life, then the medium was advised to ask for proof. The kind of information that could count as proof varied. Some mediums were satisfied with basic facts about the deceased (name, surname, birthplace, or date of death), while others requested more specific or intimate details that only the correct spirit could have known. A brand-new spiritualist trying to contact their deceased grandmother might have been advised to ask any spirit claiming to be her something very personal that only the old woman could have known.

Now, when spiritualist leaders warned of the existence of malicious spirits, they did not usually have in mind *Exorcist*-level evil, but rather the human capacity for mischief and malice, which spirits could retain and weaponize even in death. Leaders emphasized that the ghosts of departed humans were very like living humans: capable of both kindness and cruelty, plus all manner of deception and trickery. Amateur spiritualists were sternly advised to be careful what kind of people they allowed at their séances. The prevailing philosophy was that if a person of ill character sat in the circle, they were more likely to attract spirits of ill will from across the veil. Above all else, adherents were advised to keep their own intent and character pure so that they didn't draw any evil to themselves during spirit communication.

Generally, spiritualist leaders tried to walk a fine line between downplaying the danger and unnecessarily alarming their followers. For example, W. T. Stead, a spiritualist and automatic writer who is discussed in more detail in chapter 3, relayed the following communication from his spirit guide "Julia," in which she compares the hazards of the spirit-land to earthly dangers:

> *The Devil and his angels are no mere metaphysical abstractions. There are evil ones, false ones, frivolous ones on this side, as there are on yours ... But the whole question is one of balance. And what I want to ask is this, Do you or anyone else in this world ever cut off your communications with your children when they have gone into the larger life of a city, because they may bring you into the vortex of a city's temptations and the risk of evil and danger? You laugh at the suggestion. Why not laugh equally when those whom you love have passed on, not to New York, or Chicago, or London, but into the presence of God?*
>
> *I do not ask that you should open a door into your souls through which all who feel disposed on this side should enter in to possess it. You can, if you like, either on this side or on that, enter into companionship with the good or the bad. And I daresay that it is as true, on this side as on that, there is a possibility of making acquaintances who may be difficult to shake off. But so it is in London. You did not shrink from coming up to London from the country because in London there are many thousands of thieves, drunkards, swindlers, and men of evil and vicious life.*[19]

----

19. "My Experience in Automatic Writing," 48.

Séance Phenomena

The point of a séance is communication, and spiritualists recognized many different modes of communication in the context of a spirit circle; all kinds of mysterious phenomena were interpreted as messages from spirit-land. The types of phenomena most frequently reported by séance attendees varied widely over the latter half of the nineteenth century, but there were a few notable trends. For one thing, phenomena seemed to get much more dramatic in the late Victorian period with the advent of materialization séances and ectoplasm manifestations.[20] Here are some of the most common Victorian séance phenomena:

+ **Rappings or knockings**—Spiritualism began with the Hydesville Rappings, and rappings were some of the most common phenomena as spiritualism first started to take off.

+ **Table tilting**—A step up from rappings, table tilting was when the séance table began to move, shake, or spin. Sometimes, items that had been placed on the table would disappear or would be thrown around the room.

+ **Trance speech**—Channeled speech was very common at séances. The medium would either enter the trance state themselves or have someone else mesmerize them. Once they were entranced, they would channel one or more spirits from the other side.

....

20. Lehman, *Victorian Women and the Theatre of Trance*, 142–43.

+ **Automatic writing or art**—Automatism was another form of channeled communication. If a medium felt compelled to pick up a pen during a séance, they might find themselves writing messages from the dead or drawing a vision sent from spirit-land.

+ **Materialization**—In the 1870s, a new kind of séance became popular: the materialization séance.[21] In materialization séances, the medium didn't just channel the spirits of the dead but actually helped them materialize physically. Attendees at materialization séances reported seeing genuine spectral human forms appear in the séance room. These apparitions could apparently walk about like living humans, sometimes talked, and occasionally even touched people. Mediums who were able to produce these manifestations were sometimes called "manifestation mediums," and they were in high demand in the late nineteenth century.

+ **Ectoplasm**—Another relative latecomer to the séance scene, ectoplasm became a more commonly reported phenomenon later in the nineteenth century when there was increased pressure on mediums to produce some physical manifestation of the spirits they communed with. Ectoplasm was not a fully or partially recognizable human form but rather a strange gooey or filmy substance that appeared mysteriously during séances—in some cases, it oozed from the medium's nose or mouth.

---

21. Lehman, *Victorian Women and the Theatre of Trance*, 142.

- ✦ **Spirit photography**—Partially materialized spirits might not be visible to the naked eye but could still be captured by a camera. Victorian spiritualists loved spirit photography, and some mediums held séances specifically in the hopes of getting a good photograph of a spectral form.

- ✦ **Miscellaneous phenomena**—There were plenty of phenomena that didn't fit in the previous categories. Victorian spiritualists also reported: unexplained breezes, flickering lights and candle flames, strange smells, visions, ghostly orbs, and musical instruments suddenly playing themselves.[22]

A Note on Spiritualist Publications

There was a dizzying array of spiritualist books, pamphlets, journals, and magazines published during the nineteenth century. One of my favorites, a late Victorian journal titled *Borderland*, is a particularly important source for this book and you'll find it referred to frequently. *Borderland* was a British journal, but spiritualist publications flourished on both sides of the Atlantic, and some of the longest-running and most prolific were American. *The Banner of Light*, which began publication in 1857, was based in Boston and churned out weekly spiritualist news and advice for fifty years. The primary sources referred to in this book barely scratch the surface of the extraordinary expanse of spiritualist writing we have inherited from the nineteenth century.

....
22. Oppenheim, *The Other World*, 8.

Fascinating Figures

The Victorian era was awash in spiritualists and occultists of all stripes; the following are a few prominent figures whose life and work might be of particular interest to readers.

Emma Hardinge Britten (1823–1899)

Emma Hardinge Britten was born in London in 1823. From an early age, she reportedly showed evidence of psychic giftedness. As a child, she could intuit the thoughts of those around her and predict events before they came to pass. Before discovering spiritualism, Britten explored London's underground occult scene but fell afoul of some dangerous characters and had to extract herself; Britten then left the United Kingdom and traveled to the United States, where she discovered spiritualism. Britten's exploration of spiritualism gave her the opportunity to hone her talents and teach others how to develop their own psychic abilities. She quickly became one of the most prolific and authoritative writers of the spiritualist movement; her books and articles on the formation of spirit circles, the practice of mediumship, and the powers of the mind are some of the most fascinating relics of spiritualism's heyday. Britten was an avid supporter of Abraham Lincoln and a champion of women's rights. She traveled widely on the trance lecture circuit, remaining an ardent spiritualist until her death in 1899.[23]

Daniel Dunglas Home (1833–1886)

The famous Scottish American spiritualist Daniel Dunglas Home was another medium who claimed psychic abilities at a young age.

....

23. Georgina Byrne, "Britten [née Floyd], Emma Hardinge," *Oxford Dictionary of National Biography*, October 4, 2012, https://doi.org/10.1093/ref:odnb /70567.

As a child, Home unnerved the adults around him by claiming to be visited by the spirits of recently deceased acquaintances. When Home was seventeen, the house where he lived with his aunt seemed to show signs of a haunting or possession; reportedly, there were frightening noises and furniture that moved by itself. Home's aunt, already unnerved by her young nephew, accused him of having brought the devil into her home and kicked him out.[24] Despite this rocky start to his career, Home went on to become one of the most celebrated mediums of the nineteenth century. His séances were noted for their wide variety of phenomena: rapping, table tilting, spirit lights, spectral manifestations, and even auditory phenomena. Home toured internationally and ultimately worked his way into the upper echelons of society. He held séances for various European royalty and married the goddaughter of the tsar of Russia. For readers interested in delving into the life and times of the archetypical Victorian medium, D. D. Home makes an excellent subject.[25]

Sir Arthur Conan Doyle (1859–1930)

Yes, *that* Sir Arthur Conan Doyle. Humans contain multitudes, and that's certainly evident in the life and work of Doyle, who made literary history writing about Sherlock Holmes. Though Doyle's famous protagonist is an eminently rational detective who can always find a reasonable explanation for everything, Doyle himself was an ardent spiritualist who passionately defended the movement from its many critics. Doyle studied every facet of the supernatural. He was fascinated by the idea of ghosts, mediumship, telepathy, and even the existence of fairies. While Doyle has always been most famous for

....

24. Doyle, *The History of Spiritualism*, 189–90.
25. Alan Gauld, "Home, Daniel Dunglas," *Oxford Dictionary of National Biography*, September 23, 2004, https://doi.org/10.1093/ref:odnb/13638.

his Sherlock Holmes stories, he also wrote extensively about spiritualism and the supernatural. Two of his nonfiction books, *The Coming of the Fairies* (1922) and *The History of Spiritualism* (1926), are important sources for this book.[26]

Try It Yourself

For readers who want to conduct an experiment in Victorian-style spirit communication, I've provided guidelines for a traditional spirit circle. The guidelines are an amalgamation of what I've learned reading countless spiritualist publications, but they draw particularly heavily from Emma Hardinge Britten's wonderful instructional booklet: *Rules to Be Observed When Forming Spiritual Circles*, which was published in 1887. However, not everyone has spiritualist-curious friends, so I've included a solitary séance option too. The solitary séance is somewhat anachronistic; for Victorians, the communal aspect of a spirit circle was very important. Nevertheless, I tried to take the themes and essence of a traditional Victorian séance and distill them into an interesting solitary experiment that retains the spirit of a nineteenth-century circle.

Note: Modern practitioners of spirit communication advise that anyone attempting a séance begin with a ritual or request for protection (setting the intention that only benevolent spirits will come forth) and finish by bidding the spirit-realm farewell, dismissing all spirits, and closing all lines of communication.

....

26. Owen Dudley Edwards, "Doyle, Sir Arthur Ignatius Conan," *Oxford Dictionary of National Biography*, September 23, 2004, https://doi.org/10.1093/ref:odnb/32887.

Hold a Traditional Spirit Circle

The first step to holding a séance is to carefully select the participants. Nineteenth-century spiritualists believed that spirit communication required a certain magnetic or chemical balance among the people present at the séance table. Many spiritualist books and articles divided people into "positive" (or "active") temperaments and "negative" (or "passive") temperaments. The negative temperament tended to be associated with women, and it was also considered the ideal personality type for a medium. The positive temperament was considered more masculine and less innately mediumistic. Victorian séance guidelines suggested that people strive for a circle composed of half negative and half positive temperaments to achieve the perfect "magnetic" balance and ideal conditions for successful spirit communication. Some mediums would have the séance attendees sit around the table in an alternating pattern, alternating according to either personality type or gender, to enhance this magnetic positive-negative charge.

In our modern world, that sort of thing could quickly become problematic; we no longer have a purely binary understanding of gender identity, and people are unlikely to appreciate being sorted according to whether their personality type is positive or negative. So, rather than organizing the attendees according to some binary characteristic, you might just strive for an overall sense of balance, or harmony, in your group.

Three to twelve people is the ideal size for a séance, and the spiritualists tended to prefer even numbers of people. It was also advised that no more than two fully developed mediums attend the same circle together since their energy might overpower the rest of the table, throw off the balance, and actually inhibit spirit communication.

Whomever you decide to invite, have a conversation with them beforehand regarding your goals for the experience. Is this a fun Hallowe'en party activity for you, or are you really trying to recreate the conditions of serious Victorian spirit circles? Is this for laughs, or do you want a more solemn and reverent mood? If you're trying to cultivate the atmosphere of a serious session circa 1878 and your friends arrive wearing *Scream* masks and brandishing a Ouija board, then there's a fundamental mismatch between your expectations and theirs, so have a conversation about what you're trying to do.

Once your participants have been selected, you can decide as a group where to hold the séance. Whatever space you use shouldn't be too brightly lit; darkness or semidarkness is better. It's preferable that you all sit around a table, ideally a wooden table (it was believed that the wood of the table could be a conduit for spiritual powers). Some Victorian mediums instructed participants to hold hands, but many preferred that the participants each put their hands (palms down, fingers spread) on the table in front of them so that their fingers almost, but not quite, touched the fingers of those on either side of them. The evening is the traditional time for a séance, but it's important that people don't come to the circle already fatigued, so don't schedule your séance too late at night.

There should be one person who is explicitly responsible for directing the séance. At a Victorian séance, this person would typically be the most experienced medium; since you're the one reading this book, it should probably be you. You should also be sure that everyone has pen and paper, just in case they feel compelled to write or draw anything during the séance. You can open the séance with a few minutes of quiet reflection, a group meditation, a recitation of poetry or prayer, or even some music that matches the mood you're trying to cultivate. Contrary to what you may have seen in films, the Victorians didn't sit in complete silence waiting for phenomena. Mediums encouraged light conversation in the circle, but only if it stayed on topic and didn't become heated.

Whether you're sitting in silence or conversing quietly, everyone at the circle should be paying attention to the room around them: observing, waiting, and listening.

Remember the phenomena listed earlier in this chapter? Turn your attention to your five senses. What do you hear, see, taste, smell, and feel? Pay attention also to your thoughts. Are you having strange, recurring, or intrusive thoughts? If your mind wanders in a strange direction, notice where it goes. Don't forget to maintain your connection with the rest of the circle. Notice the people around you and check in with them periodically.

If anyone believes that they are witnessing phenomena, then they should make note of what they're experiencing and share what they've noticed with the other members. If people get the urge to speak directly to the spirit-realm, then they can follow that impulse, though generally, the medium in charge should be the one addressing the spirits directly. If anyone becomes uncomfortable during the séance, it is important that you end it immediately. It is not appropriate to continue a spirit circle once someone has expressed that they are uncomfortable or want to stop. When you're ready to end the séance, acknowledge that you're closing the session, thank the spirits, and bid them farewell.

Traditionally, mediums suggested that if no phenomena were observed, the séance should only last an hour—of course, you can stop yours whenever you need to. Victorian spiritualists by no means expected every séance to result in observable phenomena; they believed that it took time to forge a connection with the spirit-world. Most amateur spirit circles were advised to commit to meeting regularly each week or month for at least an hour. They were advised not to be discouraged by "unsuccessful" séances with no observable phenomena, but to commit to meeting at least a few more times with the same group to see if progress could be made. If the circle was still unsuccessful after five or six meetings, then that was considered evidence that something about the balance or magnetism of the group was off. Spirit circles that had met that many times without results were advised to alter the balance of their circle somehow, typically by either removing some current members or introducing new ones.

Sit for a Solitary Séance

First, read through the instructions for the traditional spirit circle so that you understand the underlying structure and philosophy of a Victorian séance. Since this is a solitary exercise, you can skip the ordeal of deciding whom to invite, though you should take stock of your own intentions and emotional state. Do you feel balanced emotionally? Do you have energy? Find somewhere quiet where you'll be undisturbed for a while. You can certainly sit at a table, but you don't have to.

Dim (or turn off) the lights and begin by opening your session with some variety of quiet, reflective, or meditative practice. If you already have an existing meditation or prayer practice, you could begin with a meditation or prayer. Another good option is to read (aloud, if possible) anything that puts you into a peaceful, reflective, or transpersonal frame of mind. This could be poetry, song lyrics, or selections from your favorite book. For a more modern twist, you could try opening your session with a gentle and reflective yoga practice.

Once you feel calm and centered, find a comfortable seat and ground yourself by placing your hands palms down on a smooth surface. Even though you don't have other participants to speak to, you can state your intentions aloud. What do you want out of the session? Is this a simple experiment to satisfy your curiosity? Is there a specific lost loved one whose spirit you want to feel closer to? Allow a moment or two to pass, and then observe how you feel. Refer to the list of phenomena earlier in this chapter and check in with your five senses. What does the air feel like on your skin? What do you hear? If you are so inclined, you can take notes during the séance (or experiment with automatic writing, as outlined in chapter 3). If you don't want to take notes, just focus on being present. When it's time to close the session, thank the spirits and announce that the communication is ending.

Chapter 2
Mesmerism, Channeling, and Hypnotism: The Power of Trance

... history shows that in each generation there are always a few gifted with a power (call it magnetism or what you will) which if properly developed and applied will cure disease and dispel pain. The fact remains though that while many are blessed with an overabundance of this 'vital essence' but few are gifted with the power of 'transmitting' it to others.

—Dr. J. Fraser Barbrick[27]

As spiritualists gave themselves over to the shades of the borderland, bidding the spirits of the dead to speak and act through them, some investigators began to experiment with the healing and medicinal potential of mediumship. If spirits could be asked about life, death, and the afterlife, then surely, it was argued, spirits could also be consulted regarding diseases and their cures. Some spiritualists began to identify as clairvoyant physicians—mediums who consulted the spirits of the dead to diagnose and treat illness. The most successful clairvoyant healers had plenty of clients, and their

....
27. "Magnetic Healing!" *Emporia Gazette*, April 20, 1899.

advertisements appeared in many a nineteenth-century newspaper. Meanwhile, a few more mainstream medical doctors, disillusioned with mesmerism and mediumship but intrigued by trances and trance states, began to experiment with a new practice: hypnotism. However, to really understand the roots of both clairvoyant medicine and nineteenth-century hypnotism, we must first travel back to the eighteenth century, to a curious character known as Dr. Mesmer.

Mesmerism

To those unfamiliar with the topic, mesmerism might sound interchangeable with hypnotism, but they are fundamentally different practices. Mesmerism originated with the work of the eccentric German physician Dr. Franz Mesmer (1734–1815). Dr. Mesmer believed that there was an invisible magnetic fluid that moved through all human bodies and that the proper movement of that fluid was necessary for good health; according to Dr. Mesmer, disease was caused by the blockage of that magnetic fluid. In the 1770s, he began experimenting with putting his patients into trances and passing his hands over them to redirect and unblock this hypothetical magnetic fluid. Dr. Mesmer believed that he was using his own magnetic properties (or, as he termed it, his "animal magnetism") to restore his patients' well-being and re-establish the proper flow of magnetic forces through their bodies.[28] Despite the unconventional nature of these experiments, Dr. Mesmer achieved several high-profile "miracle" cures that launched his career and brought him great renown.[29]

Later in his career, when he was investigated by skeptical colleagues, it was determined that his miraculous cures seemed to

....

28. "Franz Anton Mesmer," *Encyclopedia Britannica*, May 19, 2022, https://www .britannica.com/biography/Franz-Anton-Mesmer.
29. Lehman, *Victorian Women and the Theatre of Trance*, 31–33.

mostly function by the power of suggestion. However, regardless of the underlying mechanism, the results of Dr. Mesmer's experiments in animal magnetism were often quite dramatic and made for a remarkable spectacle. People began to call Dr. Mesmer's animal magnetism practice "mesmerism," and other practitioners tried to replicate his methods. While scientists and physicians continued to debate exactly what it was and how it functioned, mesmerism quickly spread throughout Europe and all the way to the United States and United Kingdom.[30]

Trance Performance

While mesmerism may have begun as a practice intended for medical purposes, it soon became a theatrical phenomenon. Physicians who followed Dr. Mesmer's example and tried to entrance their patients sometimes found that their patients behaved like entirely different people while in the trance state. Nineteenth-century medicine was very theatrical, and it was common for doctors to hold exhibitions during which they would demonstrate various therapeutic techniques. Public displays of trance therapy became a sensation as doctors performed astonishing experiments in front of their curious colleagues. Though some patients showed no response to mesmerism, others adopted radically altered mannerisms and personalities. They spoke with new accents, answered to names that weren't their own, and seemed to channel alternate identities.[31] It is difficult now for us to know exactly what was happening during these sessions. Were some patients just playing for the audience? Was it the power

....

30. Lehman, *Victorian Women and the Theatre of Trance*, 33–35.
31. For one example of an extremely sensational case of medical mesmerism and trance performance, see Amy Lehman's chapter on the Elizabeth O'Key trance performances of 1838: Lehman, *Victorian Women and the Theatre of Trance*, 39–54.

of suggestion at work? Were some of them really in an altered state due to the influence of their doctor?

By the time spiritualist séances began to take off in the mid-nineteenth century, mesmeric trance was already a phenomenon, and the two practices, spirit communication and trance performance, quickly merged in interesting ways. Spiritualists claimed to use the trance state to allow the spirits of the dead to speak directly through them—a practice somewhat akin to what we might think of as possession, although the mediums who practiced this form of trance rarely reported negative experiences or ill effects. Often, they reported no memory at all of what the spirits had communicated through them. In many instances, the spirits channeled by mediums had well-known names: they were long-dead royalty, recently deceased politicians, or eminent scientists. Other times, they were entirely unknown—the souls of common folk from centuries past.[32]

Speaking through the entranced medium, these spirits would hold forth on political, philosophical, and spiritual topics. They also answered questions from the audience, and relayed detailed accounts of the experience of death, heaven, and the conditions of spirit-life. There were reports of entranced mediums speaking in languages that they had never learned and assuming accents that they had never heard. Audiences turned out in droves to watch spiritualists channel the wisdom of the ages, and trance speech quickly became one of the cornerstones of the spiritualist movement. Some mediums preferred to use channeled trance speech in the context of smaller and more sedate private séances, but many mediums embraced public performance and became regulars on the trance lecture circuit.[33]

....

32. Lehman, *Victorian Women and the Theatre of Trance*, 79.
33. Lehman, *Victorian Women and the Theatre of Trance*, 88.

Unsurprisingly, contemporary reactions to spiritualist trance performances varied widely. Many Victorians were skeptical of the authenticity of the performances, while a few feared that the trance performers might be channeling messages from an evil source. Some audience members were probably just hoping for an enjoyable night out that combined elements of theater and mysticism; others seem to have been utterly convinced of the power of trance.

Clairvoyant Medicine

As mesmerism and spiritualism merged into a powerful and fascinating form of trance performance, some practitioners began to rely on the guidance of the dead to administer medical advice and treatment. Such clairvoyant practitioners usually had a specific spirit control they worked with consistently who examined, diagnosed, and treated patients through them.[34] Often, but not always, this spirit guide was said to be the spirit of a deceased doctor or scientist, someone who had received extensive medical training during their lifetime. The following is one woman's account of being treated by a clairvoyant healer and his spirit guide:

> *A few days following the anniversary services of Spiritualism in Boston (in which place I was then located), I was stricken with a heavy cold which quickly developed into a severe attack of La Grippe and typhoid pneumonia. Being entirely alone in a strange city, I had no one to appeal to, but, remembering the great relief given me last summer at Onset by Oliver Newcombe Thomas, (Magnetic Healer), when almost helpless from nervous prostration, I decided to again place myself in the care of his highly spiritual control and guide,*

....
34. Braude, *Radical Spirits*, 145–47.

'Marguerite.' This good, kind spirit treated me three times a day for one week, a circumstance which Mr. Thomas assures me never occurred before, but as 'Marguerite' afterward informed me, I was so near the border land she felt it absolutely necessary to so treat me in order to keep me on this plane of action.

—Ella M. Robbins[35]

Clairvoyant physicians often treated patients who either didn't have access to conventional medical doctors or who had already been unsuccessfully treated by the medical establishment. The clairvoyant practitioners themselves often had no formal medical training; they were frequently women, who were barred from most traditional medical schools. While the medical establishment largely scoffed at the idea of women working as doctors and the public might have been reluctant to trust a female doctor, a woman who drew her knowledge from the spirit-world operated with a different kind of authority altogether. For people who had little hope of receiving traditional medical training (whether due to their gender, race, or some other factor), clairvoyant medicine was a way to both deepen their practice of spiritualism and earn a living as a healer.[36]

Hypnotism

As mesmerism became increasingly popular, medical professionals who were fascinated by trance states but skeptical that they were caused by animal magnetism or the movement of mysterious fluids began to explore a different technique: hypnotism. Although today hypnotism is often associated with the famous psychotherapist

---

35. "Magnetic Healing," 5.
36. Braude, *Radical Spirits*, 145–51.

Sigmund Freud, Freud did not invent hypnotism. The practice of hypnotism was developed by a Scottish surgeon and scientist named Dr. James Braid (1795–1860).

Dr. Braid was fascinated by diseases of the mind, and he began to develop his theory of hypnotism after watching demonstrations of mesmerism. He was not impressed by theories about magnetism or invisible fluids, but he observed that many mesmerized people did genuinely appear to be in an altered state, mentally and physically. Dr. Braid began to believe that there was a psychological, not supernatural, explanation for the existence of trance states. He tried to find a non-supernatural method that would allow him to induce the same state in his patients. The techniques that he settled on form the foundation of the practice that we now understand as hypnotism.[37]

As Dr. Braid's theories and techniques developed, he began to use the term *neuro-hypnology* to describe his field of study, which he later shorted to *neurypnology*. The term, which originates from Greek, roughly translates to "the theory of nervous sleep," but Dr. Braid didn't think that hypnotized people were asleep; he theorized that when a person was hypnotized, their nervous system entered a strange and unique state that resembled sleep in some respects but was not the same as true sleep.[38] Ultimately, Dr. Braid compiled his hypnosis philosophies and methods into an 1843 book titled *Neurypnology; or, the Rationale of Nervous Sleep Considered in Relation with Animal Magnetism*. The hypnotism that Dr. Braid practiced resembled mesmerism in that it could induce a trance state in some people, but Dr. Braid achieved that by having his patients focus on a

....

37. Alan Gauld, "Braid, James," *Oxford Dictionary of National Biography*, September 23, 2004, https://doi.org/10.1093/ref:odnb/3226.
38. Braid, *Neurypnology*, 12.

small, shiny object until they were completely entranced by it. There was no magnetism involved, and he did not credit himself with any supernatural powers.

Dr. Braid observed that different people displayed different levels of susceptibility to hypnotism. While some people were easy to hypnotize and readily entered a trance state, others were slower to respond to hypnosis and much less likely to become entranced. He was also eager to emphasize that he didn't see hypnotism as a cure-all, stating that there were plenty of situations in which it would be unhelpful, or even harmful, to attempt hypnosis of a patient. In *Neurypnology*, he advocates for the responsible and ethical practice of hypnotism, and he warns that hypnotism, like any other medical treatment, could be used to harm people as much as help them.[39]

Dr. Braid felt strongly that the healing potential of hypnotism should be investigated, but only by those he termed "medical men"— men with professional medical or scientific training.[40] Dr. Braid was probably hoping to distinguish hypnotism from the practices of mesmerism and clairvoyant healing, which were practiced by a wide variety of people, including women and those with no formal medical training. Despite the similarities between hypnotism and mesmerism, most proponents of hypnotism went to a great deal of effort to differentiate between the two fields. They emphasized that the outcomes achieved by hypnotism were non-supernatural in nature and had more to do with the mysteries of the mind than the mysteries of mesmerism.[41]

By the late nineteenth century, mesmerism had fallen out of favor with many medical professionals, but hypnotism was considered

39. Braid, *Neurypnology*, 12, 52–53.
40. Braid, *Neurypnology*, 11–12.
41. Oppenheim, *The Other World*, 254–55.

a semi-legitimate area of investigation. While mesmerism was still strongly linked to spiritualism and the supernatural, hypnotism was associated with the growing field of psychology.[42] Today, hypnosis still floats on the fringes of the modern medical field—not quite accepted, but not entirely rejected either.

Fascinating Figures

The following people are just a few of the colorful nineteenth-century characters who practiced or wrote about trance and mesmerism. If you're intrigued by mesmerism or trance healing, you might find it worthwhile to read more about one (or all) of these fascinating figures.

Harriet Martineau (1802–1876)

Harriet Martineau was a rebellious and unconventional writer and social theorist who caused quite a stir in her own day but has been underrated by many scholars since. As a passionate atheist, social critic, and advocate for the rights of women and the working class, Martineau was on the front lines of many of the great debates of her age. Given her atheistic and scientific bent, Martineau may sound like an unlikely champion of trance healing and mesmerism, but Martineau was one of the Victorians for whom trance healing proved to be a miracle cure. In 1844, after years of steadily worsening illness, which eventually rendered her bedbound, Martineau elected to undergo a course of mesmeric healing treatment. She experienced a sudden turnaround in her condition shortly thereafter and was restored to good health within a few months. For the rest of her life, Martineau attributed her rapid and unexpected recovery to mesmeric healing.

....

42. Hammond, "A Review of the History of Hypnosis Through the Late 19th Century," 184–88.

Martineau's unconventional outlook meant that she was constantly facing censure. Her atheism shocked many of her contemporaries, and her interest in mesmerism earned her double the derision. She was also almost completely deaf, which added another layer of complexity to her experience of the world. Nevertheless, undaunted by her critics, Martineau remained an outspoken theorist and writer until her death.[43] If you're interested in learning more about a compelling, complex, and contradictory Victorian woman who tried to define the world around her rather than be defined by it, you might want to learn more about the fascinating life of Harriet Martineau.

Harriet E. Wilson (1825–1900)

Harriet E. Wilson was a Black American spiritualist who cultivated a varied career as a medium, trance speaker, clairvoyant healer, activist, and novelist. Wilson was born in New Hampshire and survived a difficult early life marred by poverty, ill health, and several tragic personal losses. Despite the challenges she faced, she was a skilled writer and speaker, and she made a name for herself as a medium and trance performer. As her popularity grew, she began to deliver more political lectures in favor of labor reform and children's education; she was also one of the first African American women to publish a novel. Despite her many successes, Wilson's path was not an easy one. Though the spiritualist community was more egalitarian than many in the nineteenth century, Wilson still experienced discrimination and marginalization within its ranks.[44] Wilson is a compelling historical figure who has only recently begun to attract

....

43. R. K. Webb, "Martineau, Harriet," *Oxford Dictionary of National Biography*, September 23, 2004, https://doi.org/10.1093/ref:odnb/18228.
44. Ellis and Gates Jr. "'Grievances at the treatment she received,'" 235–41.

the scholarly attention she deserves; much more research and writing remains to be done about her life and work.

Cora L. V. Scott (1840–1923)

An American trance prodigy and one of the greatest stars of the trance lecture circuit, Cora L. V. Scott reportedly first showed signs of psychic ability at age eleven. She quickly became a regular practitioner of spirit communication, both via automatic writing and channeled trance speech. By her late teens, Scott had made a name for herself on the trance lecture circuit; she was famous for holding forth about political, scientific, and religious topics while entranced. Scott led a very unconventional and sometimes scandalous life for a nineteenth-century woman. She was married four times and divorced both her first and third husbands (her second husband died tragically in a yellow fever outbreak along with Scott's only child, a baby girl). As she aged, she used her platform to relay messages from the spirits regarding the immorality of slavery, the rights of women, and the plight of the Native Americans. Scott lived to be eighty-two and spent forty-seven years as the pastor of a spiritualist church in Chicago. In 1893, she co-founded the National Spiritualist Association, which still exists to this day.[45]

Try It Yourself: Meditate Like Doctor Mesmer

In this exercise, you'll tap into Dr. Mesmer's theories of magnetic flow and blockage with a gentle meditation and visualization exercise. Put on some comfortable clothing and sit quietly, someplace where you won't be interrupted for at least ten to fifteen minutes.

....
45. Ann D. Braude "Richmond, Cora L. V. Scott Hatch Daniels Tappan," *American National Biography*, February 1, 2000, https://doi.org/10.1093/anb/9780198606697.article.0801893.

Chapter 2

Close your eyes, if that's comfortable for you, and get in touch with your breathing. Breathe deeply, but not laboriously, and focus on each inhale and exhale.

As you breathe, envision your body humming with a gentle current—not an intense current, like an electrical current, but a softer healing current. Feel the current shift through your body as you breathe, flowing from your mouth to your lungs to the tips of your toes and fingers. The current rolls through your body in gentle waves, and it is made up of countless tiny, shining particles. They cling to each other, dancing together, as the current of light swims through your veins. This tide of particles rides with your blood cells, carrying oxygen throughout your body and keeping you healthy.

Focus and elaborate on this image as you breathe. Imagine the tiny particles swirling through the cells in different parts of your body, from the ends of your eyelashes to the bottoms of your feet. Sometimes a few particles will split off from the others and swim to a specific body part that needs attention, bringing it warmth and light and oxygen; but eventually, they always return to the rest of the current, magnetically attracted to the others.

As you visualize, pay attention to any places where the current's flow might be blocked or interrupted. Is there anywhere on your body that feels stiff, or painful, or tense? Send the swirling cloud of particles to that region, along with your breath and blood. Imagine the shining current eroding the blocks in your body, bringing warmth and fluidity. Continue the visualization until the particles have visited all the regions in your body that feel pain or discomfort. Before you end the meditation, envision your entire body coursing with a current of light, bright particles, the tide ebbing and flowing with each breath you take. For the rest of the day, when you feel tension or pain, take a deep breath, and re-envision that current flowing freely through your body.

Chapter 3
The Automatic Arts:
Pens and Planchettes

In receiving communications by automatic telepathy, you are liable to receive inaccurate and misleading statements, embedded in the midst of a mass of accurate detail ... One day last month I had a message perfectly accurate at the beginning and at the end, but in the middle there was a false statement ... interpolated apparently without any object. In that case, however, the handwriting changed, the false statement was in quite a different handwriting from the rest of the message.

—W. T. STEAD, 1894[46]

In the hands of a Victorian medium, a pen was more than just a pen; it could give voice to the dead or pluck thoughts from a stranger's mind. Automatism, the practice of creating art or writing "automatically," was one of the bedrocks of spiritualist practice. The spiritualists were fascinated by channeled communication, and automatic writing had a lot of advantages over channeled speech and trance performance. For one thing, automatic writing or art could be

....
46. "Automatic Handwriting," 341.

done entirely alone; practitioners could commune with their spirit guides without an audience. Automatic writing was also popular with psychics who hoped to hone their telepathic abilities.[47] The tremendous versatility of automatic writing is still in evidence today. Across the twentieth century and into the twenty-first, the practice of automatic writing has become even richer and more varied. Modern practitioners might attempt automatic writing for Jungian shadow work, to connect with past lives, to channel messages from deities, to record communications from their ancestors, or as a purely experimental practice to fuel their creativity.

The Fundamentals of Automatism

So, how does automatism work? In an automatic writing session, the automatist aims to write as fluidly and unconsciously as possible, without restraint and without planning or editing their sentences. It doesn't matter if there are mistakes, and it doesn't matter whether the sentences make sense. The point is to see what can be communicated when the deliberate, conscious mind is shut out of the writing process. The writer just needs to put pen to paper, clear their mind, and write. Automatic art functions the same way; the artist just keeps drawing, without trying to plan their strokes or exert any conscious control over what the piece is becoming. During the Victorian era, automatic writing seems to have been much more popular than automatic art, but both were common in spiritualist circles.

While most automatic writing was handwritten, there were other methods. One technique that was popular with groups was to use a planchette—though not in the way that you might be thinking. While modern audiences tend to think of planchettes as part of the popular spirit boards known as Ouija boards, planchettes were

....
47. Oppenheim, *The Other World*, 148.

actually in use long before the first Ouija board was available for purchase in 1890. However, some of those early pre-Ouija planchettes were constructed differently. They were roughly heart shaped and made of wood, but they were designed so that a pencil could be attached to the underside. Thus, rather than the planchette moving from one letter to another on a spirit board, the planchette could be used to write or draw freehand on paper.[48] This old-style planchette was a popular tool for automatic writing in the Victorian era because it allowed groups of people to practice automatism together during séances. Rather than each participant picking up a pencil and writing for themselves, the entire group could place their hands on the planchette, and then they could all write or draw together.

Automatism for Spirit Communication

Though automatic writing has many possible uses, most of the spiritualists who experimented with it used it for communicating with the spirits of the dead. Automatic writing was a valuable tool for professional mediums who wanted to record long channeled messages by spirits from beyond the grave. Some mediums described the experience of automatic writing as a process of dictation; they heard spirits speaking to them and wrote the words down as they came. Others reported seeing visions from the spirit-world: flashes from the life of a departed spirit, premonitions from the future, or even blurry images of the spirit-realm itself. Many experienced a kind of physical possession occurring during the automatic writing process. They described having absolutely no control over the pen and feeling as though an alien hand had seized theirs and compelled them to write. Intriguingly, many automatic writers reported that they wrote in unfamiliar handwriting while under the influence of the spirits.

....
48. Braude, *Radical Spirits*, 24–25.

Some automatists who communed with multiple spirits claimed that their handwriting was different for each spirit they channeled.[49]

Novice automatists were counseled to take the automatic writing that they produced with a grain of salt. W. T. Stead, the editor of the spiritualist journal *Borderland*, advised people to cultivate objectivity by setting aside their spirit-writings for a full month before attempting to decipher and analyze them. Much of the writing churned out by automatists was incoherent or indecipherable; the process of finding meaning amid the chaos was an art in and of itself, and new automatists were advised to be cautious in their interpretations. Experienced automatic writers warned that many of the messages obtained from the other side were incomplete, ambiguous, or corrupted—perhaps through the intrusion of the writer's conscious mind, or through the influence of a malicious spirit. Stead once told his readership to treat each piece of channeled writing as if it were an anonymous letter—in other words, to scrutinize it carefully, assume nothing, and employ a certain degree of skepticism.[50]

Auto-Telepathic Writing

Another very popular kind of automatic writing was auto-telepathic writing. Telepathy, or "thought transference," as it was called in the nineteenth century, was a highly prized skill among Victorian psychics. Many occultists believed that automatic writing could be used not only to communicate with the spirits of the deceased, but also to read the minds of living people.[51] It was common for mediums to try to read each other's minds using automatic writing. Sometimes they tried it in the context of a séance or trance; one medium would

....

49. "Automatic Handwriting," 340–41.
50. "More about Automatic Writing," 166.
51. "Auto-Telepathic Writing." 50–51.

attempt to channel the thoughts of one of the other spiritualists present at the circle. Other automatic writers attempted thought transference more informally. Stead and his assistant editor, Miss X (whom you'll learn more about later in this chapter), regularly experimented with thought transference while they worked together. They claimed to be able to communicate with each other from some distance using auto-telepathic writing.

Although thought transference wasn't supposed to involve the spirits of the dead, there were some risks associated with the practice. Even if a medium was only trying to read the thoughts of a living person, there was always the possibility that a disembodied spirit would begin to interfere with the process. In one of her columns for *Borderland*, Miss X reported a cautionary tale of a man who began experimenting with thought transference to read his wife's mind. At first, he was very happy to be filling page after page with his wife's pleasant thoughts about him. However, the messages on the page suddenly took a turn for the worse and hinted that the man's wife was having an affair. The man confronted his wife and chaos ensued. A psychical expert was consulted, and the psychic concluded that the communication had somehow become corrupted. Miss X deduced that at some point during the experiment, a malicious spirit must have taken over the communication and begun to corrupt the messages for evil intent.[52]

Fascinating Figures

Automatism appealed to all kinds of people—not just mediums and psychics but also artists, poets, and ordinary citizens who yearned for spiritual transcendence. The following characters are just three of

....
52. "Automatic Handwriting," 340–41.

the many Victorians who found tremendous value in the practice of automatic writing.

W. T. Stead (1849–1912)

William Thomas Stead was an especially colorful Victorian spiritualist who managed to find himself entangled in many of the great debates, dramas, and tragedies of his era. Stead supported feminist causes, fought against child sex trafficking, covered atrocities at home and abroad as a newspaperman, and passionately advocated for pacifism. After becoming deeply fascinated with the world of spiritualism and mediumship, Stead founded the spiritualist journal *Borderland*.

Though *Borderland* only ran for four years, from 1893 to 1897, it published a wealth of information on a variety of spiritualist topics. One of the periodical's most prolific contributors was its assistant editor, a woman who signed her columns "Miss X." Together, Stead and Miss X experimented with a variety of different psychical techniques. They claimed to be able to communicate telepathically, and they were both proponents of using automatic writing to contact the spirit-world. Stead also claimed to be in contact with a spirit named "Julia," allegedly the soul of deceased American spiritualist Julia A. Ames.

Stead died as notably as he had lived. In 1912, Stead booked a passage to New York on a brand-new passenger liner: the *Titanic*. When the *Titanic* struck an iceberg and began to sink, Stead helped other people into lifeboats and gave another passenger his own life jacket before eventually drowning in the freezing water.[53]

....

53. Joseph O. Baylen, "Stead, William Thomas," *Oxford Dictionary of National Biography*, September 23, 2004, https://doi-org.stanford.idm.oclc.org/10.1093/ref:odnb/36258.

Miss X/Ada Goodrich Freer (1857–1931)

The prolific Miss X, who was such a frequent and valuable contributor to *Borderland*, was a woman named Ada Goodrich Freer. Freer was an ardent spiritualist and occasionally shady psychical investigator. She was also an early member of London's Society for Psychical Research (established in 1882), though she was later thrown out under suspicion of fakery and fraud.[54] During her time as the assistant editor of Stead's spiritualist journal, *Borderland*, Miss X wrote articles instructing readers on the ins and outs of mediumship, automatic writing, crystal-gazing, and thought transference. She not only investigated alleged hauntings and apparitions herself but also penned guidelines for aspiring paranormal detectives. Though she was a controversial figure in the Victorian paranormal community, especially later in her life, Miss X embodies much of the intelligence, creativity, and grit that characterized many of the most passionate nineteenth-century spiritualists.

Georgie Hyde-Lees (1892–1968)

You may have heard of the famous poet William Butler Yeats, but it's unlikely that you know much about his wife, Georgie Hyde-Lees. Hyde-Lees was twenty-seven years younger than Yeats and had the misfortune of marrying him when he was still infatuated with another woman. In 1917, a few days into an underwhelming honeymoon, Hyde-Lees experimented with automatic writing. Her results were extraordinary—she produced page after page of channeled writing. Yeats was intrigued by his bride's new pastime, and he began joining her for her automatic writing sessions. The spirits

54. J. L. Campbell, "Freer, Ada Goodrich," *Oxford Dictionary of National Biography*, September 23, 2004, https://doi-org.stanford.idm.oclc.org/10.1093/ref :odnb/46548.

she channeled offered marital advice, tips for the future, and inspiration for Yeats's poems; Hyde-Lees ultimately authored thousands of pages of automatic writing, profoundly influencing Yeats's life and work.

Despite her extremely prolific writing and her great influence on Yeats's poetry, Hyde-Lees was largely overlooked by literary historians for some time after her death. More recently, literary scholars, historians, and occult enthusiasts have attempted to draw attention to Hyde-Lees's unusual life and paranormal writing practices. I have included her in this chapter because she is an excellent example of how seemingly everyday women, including those who had no desire to be professional mediums, found empowerment and a voice through channeled spirit communication.[55]

Try It Yourself

The following exercises offer options for experimenting with automatism in a way that aligns as closely as possible with traditional Victorian practices. However, you should feel free to deviate from the suggestions in this chapter as you see fit. Certainly, feel free to write using whatever medium you are most comfortable with, whether that's a word processor, pen and paper, a tablet, or dictation software. There are different benefits to different methods. Proponents of handwriting argue that writing by hand allows for a more fundamentally powerful connection between the brain and the page. On the other hand, most people type much faster than they can handwrite, and speed is an important part of automatic writing; the more fluidly you can write (without pauses to edit or rewrite), the more likely you are to produce raw and unfiltered text.

....

55. Harper, *Wisdom of Two*, 3–7.

It's also worth remembering that it was the Victorians who pioneered the use of the typewriter, and far from being convinced that technology had no value in a magical context, they were constantly trying to find paranormal or psychical uses for new inventions. Though it might feel more Victorian to you to sit down at your desk with a quill pen and parchment paper, it is perfectly in keeping with the spirit of Victorian spiritualism to use whatever modern text-producing technology is at your disposal to contact the spirit-realm. Also, if you don't write using your hands at all and instead use dictation programs, that's also a valid way to experiment with automatic writing. Victorian writers of all kinds frequently dictated their letters or other correspondence (and many automatic writers described their practice as taking dictation from disembodied spirits), so there's no harm in dictating to another person or a program if that's how you write best.

Write Automatically

For this experiment in automatic writing, take a few minutes beforehand to clear your mind. You might meditate for five minutes or just sit quietly and let your thoughts settle. Once you feel relatively calm, pick up the pen (or sit down at the word processor), touch it to the paper, and start to write. Don't think about what you're writing—in fact, try to think as little as possible. You want to try to achieve a meditative flow state, so just let your mind drift and keep moving the pen. Remember, once you start writing, it really doesn't matter if you're writing complete nonsense; the point is to press on. Victorian automatists frequently found much of their automatic writing unintelligible, but then, amid the chaos, they would find nuggets of wisdom or unexpected insight. Just keep writing.

You can keep writing for as long as you want. I recommend at least ten minutes, but it's up to you. When you're done, drop the pen, and resist the urge to read what you've written. Put it away for a few days, and *then* read it and see what you make of it. Even if what you've written seems completely nonsensical, I recommend that you hold on to it for a few months. Automatic writing is a funny practice, and you may find that sentences, which seemed meaningless at first, begin to make more sense after some time passes.

For the Victorians, repetition was an important part of the automatic writing practice. Many of them believed that beginners were highly unlikely to make genuine contact with the spirit-world in their first two or three sittings, so they encouraged newbies to try multiple times before throwing in the towel. Your experiments might produce the most interesting results if you commit to holding multiple sessions before deciding whether automatic writing is a useful creative practice for you. Try committing to holding a weekly session for a few weeks in a row, and keep your writing from each session (preferably in the same notebook or document) so that you can compare the results of each week.

Channel Blindfolded

One of the core principles of automatic writing is that the conscious mind must be quieted so that the unconscious can have its say. This holds true whether you're writing automatically to commune with the spirits of the dead or just to explore the recesses of your own mind. Victorian spiritualists warned that the conscious mind was tenacious and would constantly try to break through to influence, edit, or block the unconscious mind from communicating with the spirit-realm.[56]

Mediums and automatists experimented with all kinds of techniques to silence the chatter of consciousness. During the 1890s,

....
56. "More about Automatic Writing," 166.

some spiritualists experimented with writing automatically while blindfolded.[57] The idea was that if the writer's eyes were covered, it would be easier for them to tame their conscious mind. Our conscious mind likes to be clear and linear, and as such, it is constantly referring to what we've already written as we compose new lines. Once the mind's ability to do this is obstructed by closed eyes or a blindfold, the writing process becomes an altogether different experience, and the shades and shadows of the unconscious have more opportunities to break through.

If you are comfortable with the idea of a blindfold, you could use one (or an eye mask or very dark glasses), but an alternative would simply be to keep your eyes closed as you write. Open your session however you see fit, but close your eyes or blindfold yourself before you pick up the pen. You might want to set a timer for a relatively short period of time (maybe ten minutes or less) when you first try this exercise. It's very easy to lose your sense of time and space during this experiment, so it might help you to know that the timer is set for a relatively short time span. When your time is up, take a few minutes to journal (reflectively, now, rather than automatically) about the experience.

Make Automatic Art

If you're more artistically inclined, you might try automatic drawing instead of automatic writing. In fact, even if you are more of a writer than an artist, there might be some value in giving automatic drawing a whirl; if you're already an experienced writer, it might be easier for you to tap into something new and raw if you experiment with a different medium. I recommend pen on unlined paper. Pencil works

57. "My Experience in Automatic Writing," 39–49.
   "More about Automatic Writing," 166–69.

as well, but if you think that you might be tempted to use the eraser, stick to pen. Try to use the largest sheet of paper you have. You want to be free to move all over the page, and very small sheets of paper can be stifling. Assemble your materials, and then take a few minutes to meditate or otherwise calm your mind. Once you touch the pen to the paper, try not to lift it again. Keep the pen moving until you feel a strong sense that your work is complete.

Once you drop the pen, drop it for good. Don't start making edits or additions. Most likely, much of what flows out of your pen will look like swirly chaos. That is to be expected, and it is true of the creations of most automatic artists. Look for shapes within the swirls. Does anything look familiar? Do you recognize anything? What emotions can you see? Does your art look angry, frustrated, peaceful, or sad? Just as you gave your unconscious free rein to create the art, it's important to lean into your intuition as you interpret the art. You can try jotting down some free associations that come to you as you look at the page. What do you think the piece is trying to tell you? These notes can be as random and nonsensical as you want. A lot of automatic practice is more meaningful in hindsight, so be sure to keep your drawing and your notes on it for a while. You never know at what point in the future you might return to the art and see something meaningful in it that you missed the first time.

Chapter 4
Spirit Photography:
Capturing the Invisibles

The camera promises to be to the psychical world what the
telescope was to the starry firmament on high.
—BORDERLAND, 1894[58]

In October of 1862, a young jewelry engraver and amateur photographer named William Mumler set up his camera to take a self-portrait. Mumler was practicing his photography skills alone in his Boston studio, and for his self-portrait, he struck a confident pose, standing tall with one hand resting on the back of an empty chair. But by the time he was finished developing the photo, the chair was no longer empty. Mist seemed to have condensed to take the form of a semitransparent girl, seated in the chair with one arm resting in her lap and the other on the table. Her upper body appeared relatively solid, but her lower body was more translucent so that it was possible to see the legs of the chair through the diaphanous folds of her skirt. She looked like a girl shaped from fog. She also looked remarkably like Mumler's young cousin, who had been dead for twelve years.[59] Mumler had no way of knowing it then, but

....
58. "The Chronique of the Quarter," 400.
59. Manseau, *The Apparitionists*, 55–56.

his bizarre self-portrait was about to ignite an international spirit photography craze.

Daguerre and the First Photographs

To fully grasp the impact of Mumler's photo, it's important to remember that photography itself was still very new. The first commercially viable photographic technology was invented in the late 1830s by a French artist named Louis Daguerre. Daguerre's method captured images and imprinted their likeness onto pieces of silver-plated copper: the resulting photographs came to be known as daguerreotypes. Between the 1840s and 1860s, daguerreotypes were joined and then superseded by several other photographic technologies, including ambrotypes and tintypes. These early technologies relied on the use of dangerous chemicals and required an experienced hand. Early photographs were almost always taken by trained professionals, and they were often shot at the photographer's studio, where the environment was controlled and the subject could sit still for a long period of time.

At first, photography itself must have seemed arcane and almost supernatural; humans had finally discovered a way to freeze faces and suspend moments in time. It is easily forgotten now, in our age of omnipresent cell phone cameras and continual live streaming, that the first photographs were precious, even miraculous, and they offered the Victorians something profound: a way to peer beyond the veil and preserve the faces of their loved ones before death. So, when news of Mumler's "spirit photograph" broke in the early 1860s, even ordinary, non-spiritualist photos still had a certain mystique. The public was still getting used to the marvel of photography, and to many, spirit photography might have seemed like a natural progression for an art form that had always felt a little fantastical.

Spirit Photography Takes Off

Though Mumler was not a spiritualist when he took that mysterious picture in October of 1862, some of the first people he showed it to were spiritualists, and once they got a hold of the photo, things escalated quickly. Word traveled like wildfire, and curious strangers crowded into Mumler's studio, eager to see the photograph for themselves.[60] As public excitement grew, Mumler took more photos … and more spirits appeared. At that point, popular opinion began to diverge sharply. While some people were utterly convinced by Mumler's images, he also had his fair share of skeptics and detractors. Many contemporary photographers of the non-spiritual variety accused him of deliberately tampering with the photographic process to create spirit images.

Whatever Mumler's technique was, he was not about to let the opportunity of a lifetime pass him by. Mumler reinvented himself as a devout spiritualist and began to offer his services as a professional spirit photographer. It helped that Mumler shot his first spirit photograph in the second year of the American Civil War. The mass casualties of the conflict meant that many grieving relatives were left bereft and desperate for a glimpse of their loved ones. It wasn't long before Mumler not only had plenty of customers, but also some competition; following his lead, other photographers and mediums soon began advertising their spirit photography services.

Many spiritualists were very optimistic about the future of spirit photography. Mediums were weary of having their practices dismissed by much of mainstream science and religion. To them, spirit photographs represented exactly what they had sought all along: irrefutable evidence that contact with the spirit-realm was possible.

....

60. Manseau, *The Apparitionists*, 57.

The pictures seemed to prove that the dead, rather than vanishing into a Christian heaven or hell (or ceasing to exist entirely), cleaved much more closely to the living than conventional doctrine held. The photographs were also visual representations of the profound experiences that believers had within the spirit circle. At last, the spiritualists could capture some of the magic of the circle and publish it widely for the edification of skeptics across the world; it was the dawn of a new era in the study of the supernatural.

Theory and Practice of Spirit Photography

Even among spiritualists who were utterly convinced of the legitimacy of spirit photography, there was some debate about how the process worked. Different spirit photographers advocated different strategies for capturing the clearest and most striking images. It was generally accepted that, to get a good spirit photograph, it was best to have someone with psychic abilities present while the pictures were taken. Many spirit photographers also identified as mediums, so they were often the ones contributing both the photographic know-how and the psychic ability. However, in some cases, a professional medium with no knowledge of photography would enlist a spirit photographer to take pictures of them as they held spirit circles, channeled trance speech, wrote automatically, or engaged in any other mode of spirit communication. In those instances, it was usually the professional medium that was credited with contributing the psychical energy needed to capture images of the "invisibles."[61]

Another interesting point regards the identity of the apparitions in the photographs. People in mourning frequently sought out spirit photographers in hopes of getting some evidence that their lost loved ones were still present and watching over them; if they

....
61. "Spirit Photography," 443–46.

had spirit photos taken, the spirits were usually identified as those lost loved ones. Professional mediums were more likely to use spirit photography as an opportunity to get a visual representation of the spirits they were already communicating with. Some mediums had their photo taken by a spirit photographer specifically in hopes of capturing an image of their spirit guide. As was discussed in chapter 1, mediums' spirit guides were sometimes the spirits of dead people whom they'd known in life, but other times, they were the spirits of strangers. Before spirit photos, spiritualists had to content themselves by asking the spirits to identify and describe whom they had been in life. After the advent of spirit photography, mediums could try to get pictures of their guides, which would hopefully corroborate the details they had already channeled in séances, automatic writing, or mesmeric trance speech.[62]

Classification of Spirit Photographs

The spiritualists were always trying to organize and classify different kinds of phenomena, and spirit photographs were no exception. The following is one spirit photo classification system, roughly as it appeared in the preface of an 1894 survey of spirit photography titled *The Veil Lifted: Modern Developments of Spirit Photography*.

Types of Spirit Photographs

+ Photographs that revealed an entity invisible to the naked eye. Mumler's first spirit photograph, which appeared to show the ghost of his cousin, would have been in this category.

---

62. "Spirit Photography," 444.

+ Photos that revealed phantom objects, such as "flowers, words, crosses, crowns, lights, and various emblematic objects."[63]

+ Photos of fully materialized spirits—so, photos of spirits that had materialized and were visible to the naked eye of the average person while the photos were being taken.

+ Pictures of the double or doppelgänger of a living person (see chapter 6 for more information on the Victorian concept of a double/doppelgänger). Some spiritualists believed in a version of what we might call astral projection—the idea that the spirit of a living person could occasionally project itself outside of its body. Thus, some spirit photographers believed that spirit photography might occasionally capture images of these "living spirits"—just as it did the dead ones.

+ Photos that included forms, shapes, and figures visible only to mediums or clairvoyants who viewed the pictures. These photos were usually attempts at spirit photography that were never properly developed by the photographer, so they looked blank or blurry to the average eye but apparently revealed something to psychics that the average person couldn't see.[64]

---

63. Haweist, Taylor, and Robertson, *The Veil Lifted*, vi.
64. Haweist, Taylor, and Robertson, *The Veil Lifted*, vi–vii.

Commercial and Controversial

Controversial even in its heyday, spirit photography has had a contentious and sensational afterlife. Since the nineteenth century, many Victorian spirit photographs have been debunked by various scientists, historians, and photographic experts. Many of the images produced during the spiritualist photography craze of the nineteenth century appear to have been the result of deliberate tampering on the part of the photographer; quite a few were clearly produced by double exposure. However, not every spirit photograph has given up its secrets, and there are some that mystify the experts even to this day.

Many nineteenth-century critics criticized the commercialized nature of spirit photography. One commentator, writing for a humor magazine in 1874, contributed the following amusing critique:

> *There is a photographer in the city who takes "spirit photographs." If you desire a picture of yourself with a shadowy spirit hovering over you in the background, this artist will engage to produce it, with a small extra charge for the spirit. He's compelled to affix this extra charge on account of the heavy tax on spirits imposed by the United States Government. He keeps an excellent assortment of spirits constantly on hand, and is prepared to furnish any one with a grandmother, favorite child, or deeply-mourned mother-in-law just as he may prefer.*[65]

---

65. "Getting a Spirit Photograph," 14.

Other Eerie Images

Spirit photos were not the only genre of uncanny photography in the Victorian era. Postmortem photos and so-called hidden mother photos were also relatively common during the period, and both were arguably even more unsettling than spirit photography.

Postmortem Photography

Though postmortem photography and spirit photography were distinctly different genres, it's interesting to note that both peaked in popularity at around the same time, in the latter half of the nineteenth century. Life expectancies were lower in the Victorian era than they are now, due in part to much higher child mortality rates. For families that had suffered the devastating loss of a child, postmortem photography offered an opportunity to preserve the likeness of their loved one. Not all postmortem photographs were of children, but the high child mortality rate was a major factor in the desire for postmortem pictures.[66]

To our modern eyes, Victorian postmortem photography might seem like a morbid and aberrant fad, but it's important to remember that those earliest photographs were rarities and luxuries. Photography was not financially accessible for many families, and so, for a Victorian family with six young children, it would not have been practical or economical to photograph each child regularly; that would have been far too many photographs and far too much money. Instead, if Victorian parents lost a child, they paid for photographs of that child so that they would still be able to see the little one's beloved face years after they were laid to rest.

....
66. Linkman, "Taken from Life," 312.

It is striking that two of the most distinctive forms of Victorian photography, postmortem and spirit photography, were both different manifestations of the same goal: to preserve a sense of connection with the dead. For the Victorians, death and photography were inextricably linked. Photography was a stand against death—a way to preserve forever a soul taken too soon or capture evidence of life beyond the veil.

Hidden Mother Photography

While so-called hidden mother pictures were not a genre of spiritualist photo, they must be in the running for some of the creepiest photos taken during the Victorian era. If you've ever looked up scary Victorian photography or perused a gallery of strange old photos, it's possible that you've seen some nineteenth-century pictures of very young children clearly held, or supported, by a person hidden entirely behind a sheet. The person behind the sheet was usually the baby's mother, who didn't want to appear in the picture but needed to keep the child still and supported for the photo. In a few instances, the hidden mother photo combined with the genre of postmortem photography; sometimes, the hidden mother was needed not to contain a fidgeting and squirming living child but to support or hold a deceased one. These photos were not supernatural or spiritualist, but they are some of the eeriest photos to come out of the Victorian era, and there is something powerfully symbolic about the figure of the vanishing, disappearing, or hidden Victorian mother.[67]

....
67. Cook, "Hidden Mothers."

Fascinating Figures

Spirit photography attracted everyone from artists to fraudsters to true believers. The following are three artistic mystics who explored photography's spiritual side.

William Mumler (1832–1884)

William Mumler: enterprising businessman, creative visionary, or unrepentant con artist? The father of spirit photography wore many hats and earned many epithets during his tenure as one of the most famous and controversial spirit photographers of the Victorian era. Mumler's spirit photography career was a wild ride from beginning to end, and it concluded with him in a state of semi-disgrace after he was charged with faking spirit photos and defrauding his customers (he was ultimately acquitted, but his reputation never fully recovered). Mumler produced many spirit photos over the course of his career, but one in particular remains famous to this day. In 1872, the grieving Mary Todd Lincoln, widow of President Abraham Lincoln, visited Mumler's studio to have her picture taken. Mrs. Lincoln had been interested in spiritualism for some time, and she had heard stories about Mumler's work. For his part, Mumler didn't disappoint the former first lady; when he developed his portrait of Mrs. Lincoln, there was a ghostly figure bearing a striking resemblance to Abraham Lincoln looming behind her. That photograph, allegedly depicting Lincoln's ghost watching over his widow, is one of the most famous spirit photographs ever taken.[68]

....
68. Manseau, *The Apparitionists*, 308.

Georgiana Houghton (1814–1884)

The British spiritualist Georgiana Houghton made a name for herself as a professional medium, a passionate (if critically panned) automatic artist, and an important spiritualist writer. Houghton saw photography as a technology with great paranormal potential; she experimented with it extensively and, in 1882, published a fascinating book titled *Chronicles of the Photographs of Spiritual Beings and Phenomena Invisible to the Material Eye*. The book contains a number of spirit photographs, including some featuring Houghton as the sitting medium, and is a treasure trove of Victorian spiritualist thought. In addition to whatever abilities Houghton brought to bear at the séance table, she was also a presentient painter who anticipated the advent of abstract art by decades. Though the abstract paintings that she created as channeled art during her communions with the spirit-world were poorly received in the 1800s, they are now evidence that Houghton was an artist well ahead of her time.

Julia Margaret Cameron (1815–1879)

Julia Margaret Cameron was not technically a spirit photographer, but her photos were saturated with their own blend of nineteenth-century magic and mysticism. A wealthy wife and mother, Cameron didn't have to rely on photography for her income, which allowed her to freely execute her own creative vision. Her images channeled a kind of Pre-Raphaelite reverence for myth and legend. Arguably one of the world's first fantasy photographers, Cameron enlisted friends and relatives to dress up and pose as legendary characters like Merlin, Lancelot, and Guinevere. Cameron's photos are extremely distinctive: they have a soft, fuzzy, slightly unfocused quality that gives them the aura of a painting.[69] Though Cameron was never a spirit photographer in the conventional sense, she explored the mystical side of photography as thoroughly as any spiritualist.

Try It Yourself

In the following pages, there are two different kinds of exercises outlined. First, I offer a few suggestions for exploring the spirit and mindset of Victorian spirit photography. Then, for those of you who are up for a road trip, I list a few museums and exhibits, in the United States and the United Kingdom, that encourage people to confront their own mortality and explore their own attitude toward death.

Look with a Different Lens

This activity is an exercise in interpretation. While photographic technology has evolved drastically since the nineteenth century, some things never change; people are still transfixed by the orbs, aberrations, and artifacts that can appear during the photographic process. Photographs can capture the truth, they can capture a lie, and they can act as a kind of Rorschach test—forcing the viewer into the depths of their own psyche to interpret particularly perplexing photographic anomalies. Have you ever seen a photo that haunted you? Maybe a photo you took yourself, a family photo from before you were born, or a famous shot by a photojournalist?

At their heart, and from their beginnings, photographs are uncanny. While it is uncommon to discover an entire phantom figure

....

69. Helen Barlow, "Cameron [née Pattle], Julia Margaret," *Oxford Dictionary of National Biography*, September 23, 2004, https://doi.org/10.1093/ref:odnb /4449.

in a photograph, many photos have something odd about them. Perhaps someone in the photo looks radically unlike themselves, there's a shadow that seems to have no source, or something in the background forms an unsettling shape or pattern. Can you think of a photo like that? You can pick one of the many weird photographs circulating online, but this exercise might prove more interesting if you choose a photo with personal significance. Do you have a blurry picture saved to your cell phone that makes you look like some alien creature? Is there a strange family photo that never fails to make you laugh because of how bizarre it is?

Instead of deleting or discarding these photos, spend some time with them. In our era, with people jaded by almost two centuries of photography and constantly on the lookout for deepfakes or photo filters, we have lost the mystical lenses of our ancestors. We are numb to the wonder of photography, slow to see the magic, and quick to scroll through a legion of digital photos that we deem inadequate in our quest for the perfect selfie. What if we look beyond the literal? What if we look for the figurative, the metaphor, the message? Rather than assume that every odd feature in a photograph is just a trick of the light, why don't you take a moment to explore the associations, the symbolism, and the figurative language of the photo? Instead of explaining away the strangeness (Aunt Mary just blinked at the wrong time, Julia was jumping up and down, Sam must have been standing in the shadows, etc.), ignore the cause and focus on the effect. What do you *see*? If you assume that the photo has some meaning or message, then what is the message? Consider journaling about your interpretation of the photo.

If you really can't find a photo to use for this exercise, you can always get behind the camera yourself and create one. There are many ways to go about taking particularly psychically suggestive photos. First, you can try taking a picture in suboptimal lighting conditions.

All kinds of strange things show up when you're working either in low light or very sunny conditions. You might get lens flares, strange shadows, and all manner of optical illusions. If you love the fey and other nature spirits—the Victorians certainly did—you might head to whatever patch of wilderness is closest and see what faces emerge from the trees (chapter 7 has more information about Victorian fairies and fairy photography). Alternatively, you can stay closer to home and just find some interesting abstract shapes and patterns in the world around you. Try taking a photograph of some organic matter. You could point your camera at a mound of dead leaves—or stand under a big tree and point the lens up for a striking view of the branches from below. Don't look at your pictures right away. With digital photography, it can be tempting to examine your photos immediately but consider waiting. Allow a few days to pass, then channel your inner Victorian and look for the magic. Look for patterns, shapes, and flaws; explore how the photographs make you feel.

Sit for a Psychic Portrait

Recruit a creative friend to take your photo. You could stage a séance (using the instructions in chapter 1) while your friend takes pictures, or you could ask your friend to photograph you as you meditate or try automatic writing. You might not get any interesting photos, but you should feel free to experiment and take risks with these shots. You and your friend can play with lighting, distance, and angles; don't be afraid to use mirrors and other reflective surfaces. If you get some compelling shots, journal about what you see in them.

Try Some Newfangled Technology—Or Wrangle an Antique

It's not easy to recapture the magic of those early years of photography, when a camera was an arcane innovation, the ultimate uncanny technology. However, if you'd like to try, my suggestion is that you get out of whatever photographic rut you might have settled in and experiment with equipment that you've never used before. If you're most experienced with a cell phone camera, see if you can borrow a polaroid-style camera that produces tiny prints on the spot (yes, they still make them!). If you have a fancy new camera that you're very attached to, try digging your parents' decades-old camera out of the attic and see what happens. You might find the most potential for enchantment when you barely know how to operate the camera you're using (it worked for many of the Victorians!). If you have the space, the time, and the equipment, you could even try learning to develop your own photos. Whatever technology you decide to use, remember that the tech, however clunky or counterintuitive, is not working against the magic—it is the magic.

Journey into Death

In lieu of an exercise outlining the practice of postmortem photography, I've instead listed a few museums where you'll have the opportunity to examine your own relationship with, and response to, death. The Victorians, so squeamish about so many things, were more in touch with the reality of mortality than we are today. We have done away with mourning periods and mourning attire, most of us do not tend our relatives' bodies after death, and we are less likely to be the ones caring for our relatives when they become seriously ill. While most of us do not want to be morbid and morose around the clock, there are disadvantages to being completely alienated from the realities of sickness, death, and dying. It can hinder our ability to empathize and be compassionate people, and both the dying and the bereaved can feel invisible in a society that likes to pretend grief and death don't exist.

The sites I've listed are all very different, but each offers opportunities for learning and reflection. You know your own comfort level best, so do your own research on these sites before scheduling a visit. If, through your own research, you get the impression that a trip to one of these locations would genuinely distress you, then you should certainly skip the visit. There's a difference between exploring your attitude toward death and traumatizing yourself—you should never feel obligated do the latter. Please also be sure to check online for the most up-to-date information on closures and visiting hours. If none of the museums listed are accessible to you, you could instead visit a local cemetery or memorial site for some quiet contemplation.

The Mütter Museum

The Mütter Museum in Philadelphia, Pennsylvania, is a powerful piece of the past, a shard of the Victorian macabre lodged in the center of a modern city. The museum was founded in 1859 after physician Thomas Dent Mütter donated his entire collection of human skeletons, wet specimens, and medical instruments. It is now one of the most famous medical pathology museums in the world, though it is certainly no place for the squeamish or the faint of heart. It does provide a fascinating glimpse into the history of Victorian era medicine, and if you're intrigued by how Victorians thought about death, disease, and the body, then this museum might be worth a visit.

The National Museum of Funeral History

The National Museum of Funeral History is in Houston, Texas, and boasts the largest collection of funerary artifacts in the United States. The NMFH's *History of Embalming* exhibit traces the practice of embalming from ancient Egypt to the present day with a special focus on American embalming practices in the 1860s. The

Historical Hearses exhibit includes nineteenth-century funeral carriages. There are also special collections related to famous historical funerals. Funeral customs reveal a lot about a culture, and the NMFH is likely worth a visit for those who prefer less grisly exhibits but do want to learn about historical and societal attitudes toward death, dying, and funerals.

Barts Pathology Museum

If you are fascinated by antique anatomical specimens, diseased organs suspended in jars of off-color liquid, or other gruesome medical artifacts, then you might learn a lot at the Barts Pathology Museum in London. The Barts Pathology Museum is part of Saint Bartholomew's Hospital, a shockingly ancient teaching hospital located in central London. Saint Bartholomew's Hospital was originally established in 1123, and the pathology museum was opened seven centuries later, in 1879, during Victoria's reign. The museum's original purpose was to be a teaching collection for Victorian medical students, who could visit the pathology museum to learn about anatomy and disease. The museum eventually fell into a state of disrepair in the mid-twentieth century, once it was no longer being used by medical students, but it has since been restored and is a fascinating place to probe Britain's history with death, medicine, and the body. The museum also has literary pedigree—when Sir Arthur Conan Doyle's famous duo, Sherlock Holmes and Dr. Watson, first meet each other and team up in *A Study in Scarlet* (1887), their first meeting occurs at Barts.

Note: Currently, the museum is not open daily, but it can be visited by appointment and during special events hosted by the museum.

Museum of Witchcraft and Magic

The Museum of Witchcraft and Magic, located in the town of Boscastle in Cornwall, England, is not specifically focused on death or funerary customs, but its collections include some more macabre items, such as bones and wet specimens. The collections are also just generally fascinating and include a lot that might be of interest to readers of this book, including artifacts related to nineteenth-century occultism and fortune-telling.

Note: Currently, the MWM is only open half of the year, so be sure to check online before going out to visit.

Chapter 5
Paranormal Investigations: Psychical Research and Occult Detectives

He visited the spot where the murder had been committed, and when he came upon the ground, or touched the instrument with which the deed had been performed, he was greatly agitated by the impression which was imparted. By means of this impression, he acquired an idea of the murderers and their movements, seized upon their trail and pursued them from house to house, and from village to village, until he actually found them.

—JOSEPH RODES BUCHANAN, 1885[70]

The nineteenth century was the era that gave us detective fiction, formal psychical research, and modern paranormal investigation. There were ghost sightings long before the Victorian era, but in the nineteenth century, a special cultural alchemy began to coalesce, and the Victorians started to do something new: they began organizing to *investigate* hauntings and ghost sightings. Simply telling stories about haunted houses or cursed crossroads wasn't enough for the spiritualists—they wanted to study and analyze paranormal

....
70. Buchanan, *Manual of Psychometry*, 79.

cases. At the same time, some professional mediums and psychics began to try their hand at solving real-world crimes—including some of the most heinous murders of their day. This chapter is all about that turn toward detection, investigation, and crime solving. How did spiritualism become so closely intertwined with criminality and detection? What techniques did amateur psychic detectives use? And what happened when the spiritualist investigators found *themselves* being investigated?

Invention of Detection

To understand paranormal investigation and psychic detection, you must first understand why the nineteenth century was such a transformative era for criminal investigation. Before the nineteenth century, there really wasn't much in the way of criminal investigative procedure. Police forces as we currently understand them didn't exist in Britain in the eighteenth century. The United Kingdom didn't get its first modern police force until 1829 when Parliament passed the Metropolitan Police Act. The Metropolitan Police Act established London's police force, headquartered at the now-famous Scotland Yard, but even those first proto-police weren't really investigators. They were tasked mostly with deterring crime or stopping it as it was happening. It was not really in their purview to engage in the complex and time-consuming process of interpreting clues and identifying unknown suspects *after* crimes had occurred. The first real detectives didn't arrive on the scene until 1842 when Britain's first detective bureau was established.[71] In the following decades, those early detectives began to explore an array of new investigative techniques. Forensic methodologies like ballistics and fingerprint analysis initially came into use during the Victorian era; around the same time,

....
71. Sims, *The Penguin Book of Victorian Women in Crime*, i-vi.

scientists and doctors first started exploring criminal psychology and profiling.

These developments in society's understanding of both criminal investigation and criminal intelligence transformed how people thought about crime in the final decades of the nineteenth century. People were fascinated by the idea of smart and sophisticated criminals who could lead the police on wild goose chases while hiding in plain sight. The titillating prospect of a violent criminal mastermind camouflaged in plain sight also fed into a paranoia that had been developing throughout the Victorian era: the fear that the neighbors' smiling faces might hide vicious, violent minds and intents. You can see this unease personified in the popular late Victorian gothic story *The Strange Case of Dr. Jekyll and Mr. Hyde* (1886), in which a seemingly respectable, trustworthy, and mild-mannered doctor becomes a violent and depraved brute by night.

With this increased suspicion (plus all the new investigative techniques and strategies) came a conviction that the world was a place that rewarded careful observation and clever deduction. The Victorians began to consider that what had once seemed random, meaningless, and indecipherable, such as the grooves on a bullet, the whorls of a fingerprint, or the ravings of a murderer, might be very meaningful indeed. Anything and everything could be worthy of investigation. This new fascination with detection led to the emergence of the detective fiction genre and fueled the popularity of fictional detectives like the famous Sherlock Holmes.

Mediums as Investigators

By now, you know that the spiritualists often framed themselves as scientific or religious investigators who probed the limits of human knowledge. But there were some spiritualists who took on a different role: that of *criminal* investigator. The link between spiritualism and amateur crime solving runs deep. In fact, it runs all the way back to the very first spiritualists and the mystery of the murdered peddler at the Fox farmhouse.

Inquiries at Home: Investigating Spiritualism's First Haunted House

While many authors and historians have written about the significance of the Fox farmhouse as the birthplace of spiritualism, the fact that there was a full-blown murder mystery playing out on the property for decades is sometimes overlooked. When the Fox sisters began their experiments in spirit communication, they allegedly made contact with the spirit of a peddler who claimed to have been murdered and then buried in the cellar some years before the Fox family moved in. The neighborhood was so intrigued by the occurrences at the Fox house that several neighbors dug around in the cellar, looking for any evidence of a human burial.[72] They found bone fragments that they thought were consistent with human bones but discovered no undeniable proof that a murder victim had ever been interred in the cellar. There was a lot of local conjecture about who might have been responsible for the murder of the peddler, though no conclusive evidence of either a murder or a peddler, let alone a murdered peddler, was ever discovered.

Meanwhile, the Fox sisters launched their careers, became famous mediums, and then burned out just as dramatically as they had started out. At the height of their popularity, the Fox sisters were extremely successful. However, as the years passed, Margaretta and Catherine began to struggle with alcoholism, financial issues, and other personal problems. By the 1880s, both had been widowed and were in dire financial straits. A reporter who wanted an exclusive story paid them a sum of money to confess to fraud and recant

....
72. Doyle, *The History of Spiritualism*, vol. 1, 55–68.

their spiritualist beliefs. The confession of the Fox sisters in 1888 caused an uproar in the spiritualist community, and both Margaretta and Catherine died destitute within a few years of their very public disgrace. Nevertheless, despite the rather dishonorable fate of the legendary Fox sisters, the old Fox property retained a certain arcane mystique. People still visited it, told stories about it, and wondered about that apocryphal peddler. Many spiritualists maintained that the Fox sisters' mediumship had been genuine and that their confessions were false.

In 1904, children playing in the cellar of the Fox house discovered a bundle of bones in the walls of the home. The news was welcomed by the spiritualist community, which saw it as evidence of the authenticity of the Fox sisters' early spirit communications.[73] Later, upon inspection, the bundle was revealed to consist primarily of a mix of chicken and other animal bones; there was no evidence that any of the bones ever discovered in the cellar belonged to a nineteenth-century peddler.

Though plenty of modern mediums steer clear of murder and mayhem, there is an undeniable link between spirit communication and criminal investigation. Perhaps it's because spirit communication is about giving voice to the voiceless, and murder victims are badly in need of a voice. Whatever the connection, the Fox sisters were far from the only Victorian spiritualists to embroil themselves in murder investigations.

Psychometry and the Murder of Mary Stannard

If you've ever watched a movie or documentary in which a psychic solves a murder by touching objects belonging to either the victim or the killer, then you're already familiar with the field of psychometry.

....

73. Doyle, *The History of Spiritualism*, vol. 1, 69–71.

The theory underlying psychometry is that energetic echoes of the past are preserved in objects. In particular, it's the belief that items of significance to a person will capture traces of that person's essence, allowing anyone skilled in psychometry to "read" the object psychically and intuit details about the object's owner. Psychometry was a very popular mode of clairvoyance during the Victorian era, and many nineteenth-century psychics tried to cultivate the gift.

You don't need to be a deeply spiritual person to sense a little bit of soul in the objects we surround ourselves with. Your father's record collection, your grandparents' wedding rings, your sixth-grade journal—all kinds of items and mementos can send us traveling nostalgically backward in time, surface a traumatic memory, or remind us of a truth long forgotten. Using psychometry, Victorians sought to trigger those kinds of associations and recollections but with objects that they themselves had no personal memory of. Instead, they attempted to gain insight about the object's previous owners through a clairvoyant reading of the object. Unlike most of the other divinatory arts practiced during the Victorian era, psychometry was focused on uncovering the past rather than glimpsing the future. Psychometry's orientation toward the past is a big part of why the technique has become so closely associated with psychic detection and crime solving.

The term *psychometry*, which loosely means "soul-measuring," was first used in 1842 by the American doctor and psychometry pioneer Joseph Rodes Buchanan (1814–1899). Buchanan was the author of one of the first major psychometry texts: *Manual of Psychometry: The Dawn of a New Civilization*, published in 1885. In his book, Buchanan described the past as being "entombed" in the present and compared the reading of objects through psychometry to a geologist's study of the past using fossils.[74] His words conjure up images

----

74. Buchanan, *Manual of Psychometry*, 73.

of memories embedded in antiques like ammonites in limestone. At the time, there were some academic geologists who attempted to use psychometry to read much older natural artifacts, such as rocks and fossils. One particularly creative psychic geologist was William Denton (1823–1883), who believed that psychometry could be used by geologists and paleontologists to get flashes of knowledge about prehistoric times. Denton was also convinced that psychometry was key to both solving and preventing crime, as he described vividly in his own book about psychometry:

> *Psychometry will yet be employed for the discovery and prevention of crime. In its presence, and it is omnipresent, the faintest whisper is loud as the rolling thunder; and there is no cunning that can conceal an evil deed from its eye; its very commission is its publication. It is a mistake, in more senses than one, to suppose that "dead men tell no tales." Their very bone-cells contain the record of every deed committed and every outrage suffered. The dungeon hears and treasures every sigh of tyranny's victim, and the ashes of the martyrs contain the story of their wrongs. It has been said that the face of the murderer has been found daguerreotyped on the pupil of the eye of his victim. Whether this is true or not, in the sense of ordinary vision, it is certainly so as far as psychometric vision is concerned.*[75]

In fact, Denton did get the opportunity to utilize his psychometric skills for crime fighting, some fifteen years after the publication of his book, when a young woman named Mary Elizabeth Stannard was murdered. Stannard was found dead on September 3,

....
75. Denton and Denton, *The Soul of Things*, 287–88.

1878, in Rockland, Connecticut. She was only twenty-two-years-old, and she had been poisoned and then stabbed. The Stannard murder generated quite a bit of attention, in part because a lot of people were confident that they knew who was responsible for Stannard's death. Mary Stannard had been having an affair with an older, married minister named Herbert Hayden. Just before her death, Stannard had informed her sister that she was pregnant by Hayden and that she was going to meet him in the woods to talk about it—soon afterward, she was murdered. The consensus opinion was that Hayden had killed her to cover up the pregnancy, but unfortunately, there wasn't a lot of hard evidence tying him to the crime.[76]

Denton, perhaps seeing this as the perfect opportunity to prove the value of psychometry in tricky criminal cases, asked for a personal belonging of Stannard's. A lock of her hair was mailed to him, and he subjected it to psychometric and clairvoyant examination. Ultimately, Denton also pointed the finger at Hayden. According to Denton, the psychic evidence was very clear: Hayden had seduced and then murdered poor Mary Stannard.[77] Unfortunately, none of the evidence, psychic or otherwise, was enough to get Hayden convicted. Hayden's trial ended in a hung jury, and he walked free; Mary Stannard's murder case was never closed.

Channeling Murder Victims: The Ripper Séances

In the autumn of 1888, London was plunged into a waking nightmare. Over the course of two and a half months, an unknown killer popularly known as Jack the Ripper brutally murdered at least five women in London's Whitechapel district. At the time, Whitechapel was a poor neighborhood of ill repute, and the five confirmed

....

76. "The Case of Mary Stannard," *Women's Journal*, October 26, 1878.
77. "Miscellaneous," *Boston Investigator*, June 2, 1880.

victims were all impoverished women, some of them sex workers. The Ripper case was one of the first "celebrity" serial murder cases. The media frenzy that surrounded the killings was nearly unprecedented in its own time and enshrined the Ripper as one of the most famous serial killers ever. While the public pored over copious sensationalized newspaper articles recounting the ghastly details of the crimes, an anonymous person or persons began sending taunting letters to the press, insulting the police, taking credit for the murders, and stating their intention to continue killing. Many historians now believe that most or even all of the letters were hoaxes, penned by individuals who had nothing to do with the murders, but the deeply sensational correspondence only compounded the public's obsession with the case. At a time when people were becoming increasingly fascinated by the process of detection, the complexity of the criminal mind, and the cat-and-mouse game between criminal and detective, the letters were fuel on a wildly sensational fire.

As the crimes escalated, a London medium, who was identified in the newspapers only as Mrs. C. Spring, led a series of séances with particularly morbid results. The first séance was held on September 6, 1888, six days after the first murder in Whitechapel and before widespread panic had begun to set in. A handful of people were present, and as the séance commenced, they witnessed Mrs. Spring enter the trance state and begin to move with strange, jerky, violent motions. She appeared to be in the throes of a violent fit, slicing at her own body with her hands as though reenacting some brutal event. The outcome of the séance was reported in the newspaper as follows:

The medium, Mrs C. Spring, was controlled, and appeared in great pain all over the body, as if suffering from severe wounds in the body; also went through the action as if cutting her throat. One of the sitters (being impressed) asked the control if it was The Spirit of Mrs Nicholls, the woman who had been murdered at Whitechapel a short time ago; and the spirit answered "Yes," adding: "The fiend! The fiend! I am not the only victim; there will be others yet. More, more, before long, and of a more brutal kind. The police are asleep…" The control also said that it was impossible for anyone present to form an opinion of her sufferings, and that she was still suffering; in fact, she could not come out of her condition at present, and asked the circle if she would be permitted to come again, and all present answered yes. The control then left the medium, wishing all "Good night," and thanking them. Mrs Spring's guides then spoke through their medium, and said: "Dear friends, just a few words to explain in reference to the last control. You need not fear for the medium, as we never permit any spirit to control our medium to do her harm. No spirit can control our medium without our permission. The spirit has received comfort and been uplifted through being allowed to control our medium to night. Your sympathies help the poor unfortunate victim; she will come to the circle again."[78]

Two days later, on September 8, the killer struck again, brutally slaying a forty-seven-year-old woman named Annie Chapman. On September 10, Mrs. Spring and her companions reconvened for a second séance. Again, Mrs. Spring appeared to be possessed by the spirit of Mary Ann Nichols, Jack the Ripper's first victim, who confirmed that her own killer had indeed attacked again and warned once more that he would continue killing until he was stopped.

....

78. "Extraordinary Revelations from the Other World," *Daily Gazette for Middlesborough*, October 6, 1888.

When the spirit was asked if the police were on the right track, she answered that they were not. In a third séance, held on September 13, the spirit of Mary Ann Nichols reportedly returned to speak through Mrs. Spring one more time; she described her killer as a muscular man with dark eyes and a dark beard.[79]

Though Mrs. Spring's séances did not help the police solve the brutal Ripper murders, they are a dramatic example of spiritualism and crime colliding during one of history's most sensational murder investigations. In an era when people were determined to get to the bottom of everything, solve every mystery, test every theory, and plumb even the secrets of life beyond death, the Ripper murders were a chilling reminder that some mysteries are never solved. Despite the efforts of the police, newspaper reporters, the frantic public, a handful of mediums, and countless amateur and professional investigators who have pored over the case since, it remains unsolved to this day.

Paranormal Investigations and Psychical Research

Although spiritualists liked to position themselves as investigators, they were just as frequently the ones under investigation. For every devout spiritualist, there were plenty of skeptics, and some of these skeptics made it their mission in life to debunk and expose mediums and clairvoyants. It was also common for mediums themselves to offer or even ask to be investigated. Often, they were trying to convince a wealthy patron or the skeptical public that their talents were genuine. If self-proclaimed mediums shielded themselves from all examinations, challenges, and skeptics, they would get a reputation for fakery; mediums needed to be able to court their skeptics, remain cool under pressure, and carry out their work under intense

....
79. "Extraordinary Revelations from the Other World."

scrutiny. They often invited their audience to test them, and the results of those tests varied wildly. Some séances and trance demonstrations were so compelling that even the most resolute skeptics left feeling transformed and convinced. Other events descended into chaos as heckling got out of control or the medium was revealed to have made a mistake or, worse, faked phenomena.

Though spiritualism generally picked up steam over the course of the second half of the nineteenth century, there were a few new roadblocks placed in its way starting in the 1880s. First of all, by the 1880s, spiritualism had officially been around long enough to see some of its champions falter. In particular, the confession of the Fox sisters in 1888 dealt a weighty blow to the movement. Additionally, the popularity of materialization séances proved to be a double-edged sword for the mediums of the late 1800s. On one hand, after three or four decades of spiritualism, the circuit was so crowded with mediums and psychics of all stripes that it could be hard to stand out, so performers who could boast actual materializations at their séances had a better shot at pulling in crowds. On the other hand, some mediums doubtlessly began to feel pressured to produce materializations and ectoplasm, even if that wasn't their personal preference; simply channeling words was no longer enough—the public wanted to see ectoplasm. Unfortunately, the more ostentatious and outrageous spiritualist performances became, the more they began to seem like tawdry exhibitions rather than serious spiritual gatherings.[80]

Society for Psychical Research

The investigative fervor surrounding spiritualism only became more intense with each decade that passed. Devoutly spiritualist paranormal investigators studied phenomena with the goal of understanding

....
80. Lehman, *Victorian Women and the Theatre of Trance*, 142–43.

spirit manifestations and communicating with disembodied intelligences. Skeptics investigated the mediums themselves, determined to expose them as frauds. This midcentury explosion of warring paranormal investigations led to the establishment of the Society for Psychical Research in London in 1882. The Society for Psychical Research was meant to be a forum for paranormal investigators of different tendencies and temperaments to share information and cooperate with each other. The hope was that the deeply skeptical and the utterly convinced would be able to work together, united in their quest for the truth. The reality proved a little more complicated, and the SPR had its fair share of quarrels and scandals in its early years.[81] However, despite the challenges, the SPR remains in existence to this day, and is now more than 140 years old.

Try It Yourself: Psychometrically Read an Object

For this exercise, you'll step into the shoes of a Victorian psychometrist and try reading an object. First, you'll need to procure an item that you don't have any personal history with. It's important that the object is new to *you* but not actually new. The item needs to have a history and story of its own. I suggest visiting a flea market, thrift store, or antique shop. Books are a popular choice when secondhand shopping, but you should consider avoiding anything that can actually be read in the conventional sense. For the purposes of this exercise, steer clear of books, letters, diaries, scrapbooks, and anything else that's literally readable. Personal items such as jewelry or clothing would be perfect for this exercise. You want to aim for the kinds of items that are used repeatedly, day in and day out. Disposable items are not a good choice, and you'd be better off with an everyday object over something so fancy that it has probably spent

----

81. Oppenheim, *The Other World*, 132–39.

most its life sitting on a shelf. Try to pick an object that feels like it's calling to you or at least genuinely piques your interest.

Once you've brought your item home, spend some time just observing it; notice what it looks and feels like. After you've gotten to know the item with your eyes open, you can close your eyes and attempt to read the object's energy, or "soul," psychometrically. You can either hold it gently in your hands in front of you, or you can touch it lightly to your forehead (Victorian psychometrists used both methods). Then, try to attune yourself to the object. Keep your eyes closed and try to keep your mind settled and still, in a semi-meditative state. Check in with your thoughts, your emotions, and all five senses. As you hold the object, how do you feel? What thoughts pop into your head? Are you reminded of anything? Does anything appear in your mind's eye? Do you find yourself noticing phantom smells or sounds? Ultimately, try to organize whatever thoughts, emotions, or sensations you experience into an overall impression of the object. If you had to use one word to describe how this object feels—beyond just the tactile sensation of it in your hands—what word would you choose? If you had to guess, what kind of household did this object come from? What kind of person owned this object before you did?

Don't forget to record your observations and experiences just in case you want to refer to them later. If you'd like to put a spin on this exercise and turn it into more of a test, you can enlist a friend's help. Ask your friend to procure an item for you: something they know the history of and you don't. Then you can compare your psychometric assessment of the object's resonance with what your friend knows of the object's history and prior owner(s).

The Invisible World: Shades of the Victorian Supernatural

Part 2

Chapter 6
Ghost-Seers and Ghostlore: From the Night-Side to the Ghost World

– GHOST HUNTING IN DURHAM –

The villagers of Birtley, near Newcastle, have been much excited of late by strange sounds heard in the house of a miner named Wild. The walls and roofs have been pierced to discover the cause, and the partitions have been smoked, but no discovery has been made. A correspondent telegraphs that he sat up with the ghost to a late hour on Tuesday night. He heard a cry at intervals—a far-away tremulous wailing sound, but saw nothing unusual. Local Spiritualists have expressed a desire to interview the "shade," but Wild has declined. All kinds of stories are afloat as to the ghost, and crowds assemble nightly outside the house.

—FROM THE PAGES OF THE *YORK HERALD*, 1892[82]

Spiritualism as it was practiced by the Victorians was a mid-nineteenth-century development, but there have likely been ghost sightings for as long as there have been humans. Not all

....
82. "Ghost Hunting in Durham," *York Herald*, September 24, 1892.

Victorians who saw ghosts were ardent spiritualists, and not all specters appeared in the context of a séance. While the spiritualists were usually eager to investigate any reported ghost sightings, not everyone who had encountered an unearthly spirit wanted anything to do with the spiritualists—as is evident from this chapter's epigraph about the unfortunate Mr. Wild and his haunted house. In this chapter, we explore the nineteenth-century ghostlore and ghost-seers that existed outside of spiritualism. The "Ghost-Seers" section details the difference between a ghost-seer and a spiritualist medium, while "Notable Ghost Sightings" explores the very dramatic consequences of some famous pre-spiritualist ghost sightings. "Ghostlore" traces the arc of Victorian ghostlore from the 1840s through the 1890s.

Ghost-Seers

Mediums were not the only people seeing spirits in the nineteenth century; there was another term sometimes used to describe a person who reported seeing an unearthly apparition: a ghost-seer. While the Victorians' use of the terms *medium* and *ghost-seer* are not always clearly delineated, Victorian authors tended to use the two terms differently. People who engaged in intentional, structured spirit communication were known as mediums. Mediums deliberately sought contact with the spirit-realm. They experimented with different methods, such as séances, trances, and automatism. They made repeated efforts at spirit communication, honed their techniques, built up their skills, and kept records of their attempts. Mediums tended to have discrete goals: specific spirits they were attempting to contact, specific questions they wanted answered, and specific abilities they were trying to develop.

In contrast, ghost-seers were people who had reported an unexpected and often quite unnerving encounter with an apparition—such as a man who saw a headless phantom gallop past him on the road late one evening, a woman who woke up in the middle of the night to find a ghostly lady in white standing at the foot of her bed, or a child who reported being visited by the spirit of a dead playmate. While mediums rarely reported being afraid of the phenomena they witnessed, ghost-seers were often quite frightened by their unsolicited brush with the night-side. Among mediums, an unearthly encounter was usually interpreted as encouraging evidence of life after death and the feasibility of spirit communication. Ghost-seers were working with an older and scarier paradigm; they were likelier to interpret their sightings as ill omens, and they were much more concerned about the existence of malevolent spirits. The ghost sightings reported by ghost-seers were often rooted in local legends. Ghost sightings could certainly happen at home, but they were also very likely to happen at crossroads, in churchyards, and other places strongly associated with myth and lore. Since spiritualists were the ones initiating their contact with the spirit-realm, they got to choose the timing and manner of their encounters, and so they were less likely to report being randomly menaced by a faceless shadow while walking back from town one night.

Notable Ghost Sightings

So, if we take spiritualism out of the picture for a moment and think only about ghost-seers, what were some of the most famous nineteenth-century ghost sightings? How did people experience apparitions and hauntings before the spiritualists arrived on the scene and radically altered the paradigm? In the following pages, I've detailed two famous early nineteenth-century ghost sightings or hauntings.

One was later revealed to have been an irresponsible hoax; the other has never been explained.

The Hammersmith Ghost (London, 1803–1804)

Of all the pre-Victorian ghost sightings, few caused as much panic, drama, and, ultimately, tragedy as the Hammersmith Ghost. In December of 1803, residents of Hammersmith, a district in West London, were traumatized by the repeated appearance of a ghostly apparition. The phantom, reportedly clad in a white shroud, ran through the streets, terrifying everyone it encountered. There were even reports that an elderly woman had been so traumatized by her encounter with the specter that she'd succumbed to shock.[83] Determined to get to the root of the mischief, some citizens took it upon themselves to patrol the streets of Hammersmith in search of the specter. Matters came to a tragic head on January 3, 1804, when a man named Francis Smith took to the streets with his gun. The newspapers described the situation thus:

> *The neighbourhood of Hammersmith has been for some time past in a constant state of alarm, on the supposed appearance of an apparition every night, as the church clock struck twelve, in the field adjoining Black Lion-Lane, which appeared as if covered in a shroud, and prevented the women and children from going out at night, and kept the men at an awful distance. After several fruitless attempts to discover the author of this phantom, Francis Smith, an excise officer, resolved to make a discovery, and for that purpose he took his fusee,[84] and after loading it with powder and ball, proceeded*

83. "Friday's and Saturday's Posts," *Hampshire Chronicle*, January 9, 1804.
84. A fusee is a kind of firearm.

to the spot where the supposed ghost used generally to make
its appearance.[85]

Unfortunately, at the same time Francis Smith went patrolling, another man, Thomas Millwood, a local bricklayer, was also on the road. Millwood was only twenty-two years old, and he was just walking home, dressed in a white jacket and white trousers, which was the standard uniform for bricklayers at the time. When Smith encountered Millwood on the road that night, he was convinced that he was staring down the Hammersmith specter; Smith fired on Millwood, killing him instantly. People came running from all over the neighborhood, and within minutes, it was discovered that Smith had made a tragic mistake.

Smith was charged with murder, and the sensational details of the Hammersmith Ghost killing were splashed across the papers for weeks. In the midst of the chaos, a local man named Graham came forward and claimed that he was responsible for the initial ghost sightings and spectral mayhem; he had been dressing up as a ghost to frighten people.[86] If Graham was telling the truth, then the Hammersmith Ghost affair, which ended in the loss of a young life, was a prank that got out of hand. The unfortunate Smith was first sentenced to death, but later had his sentence commuted to a year of hard labor. The Hammersmith Ghost case went on to have a very complicated legal afterlife in the United Kingdom—it was at the center of years of legal debate regarding the culpability of someone who kills another based on a mistaken belief.

....
85. "The Hammersmith Ghost!" *Hull Packet,* January 17, 1804.
86. "The Hammersmith Ghost!" *Hull Packet,* January 17, 1804.

Chapter 6

The Bell Witch Haunting (Tennessee, 1817–1820)

Early nineteenth-century America had its fair share of ghost legends, but few can match the truly bizarre Bell Witch Haunting. The Bell Witch Haunting, which reportedly played out from approximately 1817 to 1820 in Robertson County, Tennessee, has intrigued writers and historians for generations. The trouble began and ended with the Bell family, who had been living in their home along the Red River for more than a decade when they began to sense a malevolent presence. The Bell family included John Bell, his wife, Lucy Bell, and their six children: five sons and a daughter named Elizabeth. Sometime around 1817, when Elizabeth was eleven, the family began to report all the classic signs of a haunting. At night, the children were disturbed by what sounded like an animal scratching the floor and gnawing on their bedposts. They reported having their blankets yanked off them and their hair pulled while they slept at night. The phenomena particularly seemed to center around John Bell and, to a lesser extent, his young daughter.

When neighbors heard of the troubles at the Bell house, they came flocking to witness the phenomena for themselves, and they discovered a household in chaos. Elizabeth had begun to experience fits, during which she would collapse from shortness of breath. John reported an entire suite of maladies, including a tongue so swollen that it made it difficult for him to eat or speak. Outside of the house, there were sightings of a strange beast that could vanish into thin air. Inside of the house, there were malevolent whispers; visitors to the Bell house heard what sounded like a disembodied woman's voice muttering threats and insults. The whispering voice identified herself as the source of the phenomena in the house but gave many different, conflicting accounts of her true identity. Eventually, the Bell family and locals took to calling the entity "Kate" because that was one of the names she used. Kate was alternately described as a ghost, a witch, a goblin, and a demon.

Meanwhile, the situation at the Bell house continued to devolve. Kate allegedly taunted the family, kept them up at night, pinched and tormented the children, and threatened John's life. Eventually, Elizabeth began to recover from her illness, but John kept getting worse. On the morning of December 19, 1820, matters came to a head. No one could wake John, so one of his sons ran to the medicine cabinet to look for something to help rouse him. Instead of the usual medicines, however, the only thing in the cabinet was a mysterious vial, mostly empty, with just a little unidentified dark brown liquid remaining at the bottom. The family sent for a doctor, and as they waited, they heard Kate's gleeful voice—she claimed to have poisoned John and was celebrating his impending death. A doctor did eventually arrive, but he could neither identify the liquid nor help John, who died the next day.[87]

According to legend, most of the Bell Witch phenomena ended once John Bell was buried. More than two centuries have passed since the Bell Witch Haunting, and what really happened in that home along the Red River remains a mystery. Could it have been a prank run wildly out of hand, like the Hammersmith Ghost affair? Did someone in the house murder John Bell and cover it up by faking supernatural phenomena? If John Bell succumbed to an illness, then what was his illness? Whatever caused the phenomena at the Bell home, the Bell Witch Haunting remains one of the most mystifying episodes in North American ghostlore.

....
87. Ingram, *An Authenticated History of the Famous Bell Witch*, 181–82.

Ghostlore

The nineteenth century was a bountiful era for ghost sightings and ghost-seers, and it was also an important century for ghostlore. As is covered in more detail in chapter 7, the nineteenth century was when the preservation and study of folklore really started to flourish, and ghostlore was an important and popular subgenre of folklore. In the following pages, we'll trace Victorian ghostlore from an 1847 compendium published just before the dawn of spiritualism to an 1893 collection published at the sunset of the Victorian era.

Catherine Crowe and the Night-Side of Nature

A year before the Fox sisters began experimenting with spirit communication in their New York farmhouse, a British writer named Catherine Crowe (1803–1876) published a book intended to be a comprehensive taxonomy of supernatural beings and phenomena: *The Night-Side of Nature; or, Ghosts and Ghost-Seers*. Released in 1847, the book catalogs a cornucopia of different paranormal manifestations; the author, Crowe, was a novelist, playwright, and lover of the mysterious and unexplained. Crowe got her start as a writer penning sensational novels and short stories, but as her fascination with the supernatural deepened, she became committed to writing and publishing on paranormal topics. Crowe was fluent in German, and her first foray into paranormal writing began with a translation project: *Die Seherin von Prevorst (The Seeress of Prevorst)*. The so-called Seeress of Prevorst was a German clairvoyant named Frederica Hauffe who, in the late 1820s, became famous for her trances and visions. A German doctor named Justinus Kerner wrote a book about Hauffe, titled *Die Seherin von Prevorst*, in 1829. Crowe was intrigued by reports of Hauffe's unearthly powers, and she translated Kerner's book into English in 1845.

A few years later, Crowe made her own very influential contribution to the field of paranormal studies as the author of *The Night-Side of Nature*, compiling many supernatural tales and reports (including quite a few from continental Europe) into a single volume. Throughout her career, Crowe drew heavily on the work of German folklorists and writers, and *The Night-Side of Nature* includes several German supernatural creatures, including the poltergeist and the doppelgänger.

Since Catherine Crowe wrote *The Night-Side of Nature* right before the advent of spiritualism, she was mostly recording legends about ghost-seers: people who had happened upon spirit manifestations on dark and dismal nights. It wasn't until a few years after the publication of Crowe's book that professional mediumship really became a viable career option. Crowe described and distinguished between wraiths, doppelgängers, apparitions, and poltergeists; she discussed prophetic dreams and presentiments and included chapters on haunted houses and troubled spirits. However, since *The Night-Side of Nature* was a pre-spiritualist text, it included no mention of spirit circles or séances, which would go on to be all the rage within a decade or two after the work's publication.

Crowe's compendium of apparitions is a crucial text for anyone who wants to understand the culture of Victorian ghostlore, so, in the following pages, I've included a few of the creatures she defined and described in *The Night-Side of Nature*. For Crowe, the *timing* of a spirit sighting was extremely important; one of the organizing principles of her taxonomy of apparitions was whether a spirit was spotted before, after, or exactly at the time of the human body's death. Crowe's classification of spirits was not always clear-cut, especially since she drew on a variety of lore from across regions and time periods, but her distinction between wraiths, doppelgängers, and ghosts usually boiled down to when the spirit appeared relative to the death of its human body.

+ **Wraiths**—Wraiths were spirits that appeared to people at the exact moment of a loved one's death. Wraiths didn't usually speak or communicate in any way, but they were believed to appear to warn friends and family that a loved one was passing on. Crowe provides several suspenseful accounts of people who caught a glimpse of their loved one's face, only to later learn that person had died at the same time. Here is just one example:

In the year 1813, a young lady in Berlin, whose intended husband was with the army at Dusseldorf, heard some one knock at the door of her chamber, and her lover entered in a white negligé, stained with blood. Thinking that this vision proceeded from some disorder in herself, she arose and quitted the room, to call a servant; who not being at hand, she returned, and found the figure there still. She now became much alarmed, and having mentioned the circumstance to her father, inquiries were made of some prisoners that were marching through the town, and it was ascertained that the young man had been wounded, and carried to the house of Dr. Ehrlick, in Leipsic, with great hopes of recovery. It afterward proved, however, that he had died at that period, and that his last thoughts were with her. This lady earnestly wished and prayed for another such visit, but she never saw him again.[88]

....

88. Crowe, *The Night-Side of Nature*, 155.

+ **Doubles, or doppelgängers**—Doubles were prominent in nineteenth-century ghostlore and gothic literature. Crowe, ever a fan of German folklore, used the
German term for a double in her book: *doppelgänger*.
To Crowe, a doppelgänger, or double, was a ghostly
apparition of a currently living person, closely related
to a wraith. Instead of appearing at the exact moment
of death, a doppelgänger would appear sometime before a death or other calamity as a death omen or
harbinger of coming misfortune. Doppelgängers are a
particularly fascinating feature of nineteenth-century
ghostlore that seems to have become less common
over time. Many modern spiritual practitioners report contact with all manner of entities and spirits,
but even in very unconventional circles, it's unusual to
hear someone describe having encountered their own
doppelgänger—or indeed, to report having seen the
spectral twin of any currently living person. However,
in the nineteenth-century, doppelgängers were incredibly common in ghostlore, and Crowe devotes an entire
chapter to them.[89]

+ **Ghosts**—While there's some bleed between Crowe's
categories (since even she struggles to neatly classify the
mass of reported apparitions and specters in her book),
she generally uses the term *ghost* to refer to spirits
sighted sometime *after* the death of their body. This, of
course, is essentially what our modern understanding
of a ghost is. Crowe also tried to parse out the possible

....
89. Crowe, *The Night-Side of Nature*, 161.

motivations of various ghostly spirits: some might be troubled by violence or injustice directed toward them during their life, while others might seek the prayers of the living. The idea of a spirit that needs the prayers of the living maps onto the religious framework of some of the early celebrations of All Souls' Night (discussed further in chapter 11), when people were encouraged to pray for their beloved dead in hopes of freeing their souls from purgatory and releasing them into heaven.[90]

+ **Poltergeists**—Poltergeists were another German category of spirit that Crowe introduced and explained to her British audience. Her description of reported poltergeist activity resonates strongly with what's typically depicted in our modern media: an escalating pattern of household disruption, ranging from the mischievous to the genuinely dangerous. However, one interesting belief about the poltergeist that Crowe had was that she didn't believe that poltergeists were necessarily the lingering souls of dead people. Poltergeists, Crowe suggested, were inhuman spirits: an entirely separate class of being from a different realm, that occasionally entered the human world to wreak havoc before departing back to whatever realm they originated from.[91]

Thiselton-Dyer's Ghost World

The second text of major significance for this chapter is T. F. Thiselton-Dyer's 1893 book *The Ghost World*. Thomas Firminger

....

90. Crowe, *The Night-Side of Nature*, 383.
91. Crowe, *The Night-Side of Nature*, 431–33.

Thiselton-Dyer (1848–1923) was a British writer and curate with a passion for recording all manner of folklore and legend. In addition to *The Ghost World*, Thiselton-Dyer authored a number of other folklore collections, including *The Folk-Lore of Plants*, *Domestic Folk-Lore*, and *Folk-Lore of Shakespeare*. Though Thiselton-Dyer is not widely known today, his body of work is a treasure trove of legend and folklore.

Published fifty years after Crowe's compendium, *The Ghost World* has a lot in common with *The Night-Side of Nature*, but there are some key differences. For one thing, Thiselton-Dyer was not a true believer like Catherine Crowe. He appears to have been gently skeptical with respect to spirits and apparitions, but he was deeply dedicated to recording as many tales, legends, and supernatural reports as possible. So, while Catherine Crowe was invested in convincing her readers of the validity of ghost sightings and supernatural manifestations, Thiselton-Dyer takes a more distant and academic approach. He records the legends for posterity and, except for a few humorous comments, mostly leaves it up to the reader to judge the stories for themselves. This distinction is intriguing because it speaks to how Victorian attitudes toward ghosts changed from 1847 to 1893. Between the 1840s and the 1890s, the study of folklore and legend came to be recognized as a legitimate field. Thanks to the budding field of folklore studies, it was acknowledged that ghost legends and sightings could be fascinating culturally and historically without needing to be true or accurate. Folklorists, like Thiselton-Dyer, could write extensively about ghosts without having to come down decisively on one side or the other of the "Are ghosts real?" debate.

Below, I have included just a sample of the fascinating Victorian ghostlore assembled in his remarkable book.

+ Crossroads were rumored to be particularly supernaturally active, and some people might have avoided the crossroads at night for fear of encountering uneasy spirits wandering the countryside.[92]

+ It was believed that murderers, murder victims, and the spirits of those who died by suicide were all more likely to return to the realm of the living as ghosts.[93]

+ The first crows of a rooster at dawn were said to dissolve or banish all manner of unearthly presences—including the devil himself.[94]

+ Some old legends held that the presence of an unearthly spirit would be signaled by candle flame suddenly burning a different color.[95]

+ Saint John's eve is one of the days that is cited repeatedly in folklore as a time of increased spirit activity. Saint John's eve begins as the sun sets on June 23 and is closely associated with the summer solstice. Due to the multitude of legends about spirit activity on Saint John's eve, some people were quite superstitious around that time of year. One legend held that a person who waited at the front door of the church all night on Saint John's eve would see the spirits of those doomed to die in the coming year; it was rumored that the doomed souls would proceed to the entrance of the church in the order in which they were fated to die.[96]

....

92. Thiselton-Dyer, *The Ghost World*, 53.
93. Thiselton-Dyer, *The Ghost World*, 53.
94. Thiselton-Dyer, *The Ghost World*, 354–55.
95. Thiselton-Dyer, *The Ghost World*, 137–40.
96. Thiselton-Dyer, *The Ghost World*, 387.

+ Another midsummer legend holds that on Saint John's eve, the spirit of every living person slips out of their body and travels to the exact place where that person will eventually die.[97]

+ It was believed that some families had hereditary death omens—specific to their family line—which would appear before someone in the family was about to die. Some of the death omens given as examples include owls, banshees, and ghostly nuns and friars.[98]

+ One Highland superstition held that if you buried the boots of the dead under water, it would prevent their spirit from walking amongst the living.[99]

Try It Yourself: Read Some Victorian Ghostlore

For this exercise, I challenge you to track down and read some authentic Victorian ghostlore! I've woven the spirit and language of the Victorians throughout this book to make it as authentic as possible; however, as a Victorianist and ardent archive-diver myself, I know that there are some things that should be experienced directly from the source. Both *The Night-Side of Nature* and *The Ghost World* are in the public domain and available for free online (there are also printed editions available from various sources). Obtain a copy in whatever format works for you (digital, print, audio) and read a few pages. If you really want a feel for the rhythm and cadence of the Victorian era, you might try reading aloud. You don't need to read the entire book, just enough to get a feel for it. You may discover that, though you love learning about the Victorian period, you find Victorian language patterns and prose style deeply

....

97. Thiselton-Dyer, *The Ghost World*, 388.
98. Thiselton-Dyer, *The Ghost World*, 221–23.
99. Thiselton-Dyer, *The Ghost World*, 180.

frustrating—and that's perfectly valid. I love the Victorians, but their language is an acquired taste and certainly not everyone's cup of tea. For the purposes of this exercise, approach the text with an open mind, and give it a chance to surprise you.

Chapter 7
Fairies, Flowers, and Folklore: Natural Enchantments

Come away, O human child!
To the waters and the wild
With a faery, hand in hand,
For the world's more full of weeping
than you can understand.
—W. B. Yeats, "The Stolen Child"[100]

As technology rushed ahead, birthing a new age of trains and telegrams, Victorians reached forward with one hand and backward with the other. During the Victorian era, there was a surge of interest in folklore and legends, as well as a voracious appetite for fairy art and literature. This chapter delves into the Victorian magic of fey, folktales, and flowers: the magic of nature and place, rooted in a way of life that was fading even as the Victorians penned their fairy poems and recorded their legends.

....
100. Yeats, *The Poetical Works of William B. Yeats*, vol. 1, 39.

Folklore

In many respects, the advent of folklore studies was part of the broader medievalism that gripped the Victorians. Victorian medievalism was the nineteenth-century obsession with Arthurian legend and early British history.[101] Like the Victorian love of folklore and fairy art, medievalism is commonly understood as a nineteenth-century reaction against the explosive urbanization of the time. In Britain, from the late eighteenth century to the mid-nineteenth century, many people, whose families had for centuries lived in small rural towns or hamlets, made their way to large cities. These people moved for economic opportunity, to feed their families and survive, but their migrations also set into motion a gradual process of forgetting nature and disconnecting from the land.[102] The rhythms that had governed life in the country were lost in the city. Natural cycles that had ruled the days, nights, months, and years of rural life began to lose their meaning.

The Victorians were uneasy about this transition. They could personally see and feel all the advantages of new technologies and scientific advances—but they had a front row seat to the poison and ugliness as well. Victorian cities were polluted. The skies were dim with smoke from continuous coal burning. They had no antibiotics, very few vaccines, and insufficient hygiene, so disease spread rapidly. Factories were unsafe, the streets were dirty, and poor children were expected to work from a young age.[103] Medievalism was one way of looking for beauty in a polluted world, and the Victorians used it to lose themselves in time and revisit the magic of Merlin and the allure of fairy nobility like Queen Titania or Lady Nimue.

....

101. Alexander, *Medievalism*, xx–xxi.
102. Greenblatt and Abrams, *The Norton Anthology of English Literature*, 1017–18.
103. Greenblatt and Abrams, *The Norton Anthology of English Literature*, 1022.

This nostalgia, coming at a time when lots of newer academic disciplines (like anthropology and archaeology) were developing and solidifying, led to the emergence of folklore studies as a consolidated field.[104] The Folklore Society, Britain's first formal organization for the study of folklore, was founded in 1878.[105] A decade later, in 1888, the American Folklore Society was founded in the United States.[106] The study of folklore, the practice of discovering and recording various local legends, gave Victorians a way to hold on to the past and maintain a connection with their ancestors. It also allowed for a return to the countryside. Folklorists typically focused their attentions on out-of-the-way places: small rural hamlets and villages that seemed to have been forgotten by time. Modern scholars are indebted to those early folklorists for the care and dedication with which they preserved the stories of their age for the readers of our age.

Fairies

Fairies were at the heart of the Victorian desire for enchantment. People longed for the fairy wood of William Shakespeare's *A Midsummer Night's Dream* and the enchanted island of his romance *The Tempest*. The Victorians wanted to be bewitched, and the first folklorists and fairy historians wanted to record whatever magic remained in their time. Fairies weren't just contained to the notebooks of the first folklorists; they appeared in literature, on canvases, and in front of the camera lens.

....

104. Silver, *Strange and Secret Peoples*, 4.
105. Simpson and Roud, *A Dictionary of English Folklore*, 128.
106. Bell, "William Wells Newell and the Foundation of American Folklore Scholarship," 10.

The History of Fairies

Fairies, faeries, or the fey, to give but a few of their monikers, are a tricky group to categorize and talk about. For the purposes of this chapter, we are focusing mostly on British and Irish fairy lore, but even with that geographic boundary in place, the subject is extremely complicated. The first written record of fairies and fairy tales in England dates to approximately 1214. The *Otia Imperialia*, which roughly translates to "Recreation for an Emperor," is an encyclopedic work by Gervase of Tilbury (c. 1150–1220) that presents an array of fascinating and mythological topics.[107]

Various writers and scholars returned to the topic of fairies in the centuries following Tilbury's work, but serious attempts to categorize the various fairies and fey creatures that were so popular in song, myth, and folklore didn't begin in any serious systematic way until the 1800s.[108] In 1828, an Irishman named Thomas Keightley published a book called *The Fairy Mythology* (the book was later also published under the alternate title *The World Guide to Gnomes, Fairies, Elves, and Other Little People*). Keightley drew on many sources, including the venerable *Otia Imperialia*, and his fantastic and carefully researched catalog of fairy kind and fairy lore inspired and influenced the first generation of folklorists.

Fairy Myths and Associations

Many of our modern associations with the fey were established by the Victorian era; lots of the themes and tropes that pepper contemporary stories about fairies were already common in the nineteenth century. The Victorians thought of fairies as the invisible guardians and rulers of wild spaces (and sometimes households). Their fey, like

---

107. Schlager, "Gervase of Tilbury," 536.
108. Forsberg, "Nature's Invisibilia," 642.

ours, were by turns fierce, deceptive, alluring, seductive, terrifying, and mischievous. Halfway between trickster gods and nature spirits, these beautiful and occasionally bizarre creatures were said to strike cunning bargains with humans, lure mortals into the fairy realm, abduct children, ferociously defend wild spaces encroached upon by humans, and live alongside wild creatures such as bats, songbirds, and toads.

The Goblin Market

There was a torrent of fairy-themed art and writing in Britain during the Victorian era.[109] Many poets and authors used the Victorian fascination with the fey to explore themes of temptation, illusion, seduction, virtue, and vice. One particularly powerful example is Christina Rossetti's 1862 poem "Goblin Market." In Rossetti's long narrative poem, two young sisters are tempted by the delicious (but deadly) fruits sold by uncouth goblin men. Though all the young women in their village are warned to steer clear of the goblins and their wares, one of the sisters gives in to temptation. Rossetti's poem is a powerful blend of seductive and unsettling, sweet and sinister. In "Goblin Market," Rossetti taps into a thread that has run through many fairy stories: the idea that the fey are oddly attuned to, and often manipulative of, human appetites.

Species of Fairy

Many of the categories of British and Irish fairies described by Keightley are likely to be familiar to anyone who has read a lot of folklore, fairy tales, or fantasy novels. I've included a selection of the creatures Keightley describes, and I've tried to mix some of the more famous creatures with a few that might be less familiar.

....

109. Silver, *Strange and Secret Peoples*, 3.

Brownies

Many old fairy stories feature tales of the humble house brownie, a tiny fey creature that Keightley describes as "a personage of small stature, winkled visage, covered with short curly brown hair, and wearing a brown mantle and hood." Brownies were believed to live in the hollows of old trees, in the ruins of castles, and in the homes of humans. They tended to grow very attached to specific families and would live with those families for generations, tending to various household chores and looking after the land. The brownie would stay with the family provided they weren't offered any overly generous gifts; apparently, brownies had quite a bit of pride and were insulted by anything they interpreted as payment. Keightley cautions the reader never to openly offer a brownie a present but rather to leave a bowl of cream or a fresh honeycomb in a quiet corner somewhere so that the brownie can help themselves in private.[110]

The Grant

Another fascinating creature described in Keightley's book of fairy mythology is the creature known as the Grant, which Keightley took straight from the *Otia Imperialia*:

> *There is ... in England a certain kind of demon whom in their language they call Grant, like a yearling foal, erect on its hind legs, with sparkling eyes. This kind of demon often appears in the streets in the heat of the day, or about sunset. If there is any danger impending on the following day or night, it runs about the streets provoking the dogs to bark, and, by feigning flight, draws the dogs after it, in the vain hope of catching it. This illusion warns the inhabitants to*

----

110. Keightley, *The Fairy Mythology*, 357–60.

beware of fire, and the friendly demon, while he terrifies those who see him, puts by his coming the ignorant on their guard.[111]

Portunes

Less famous than their pixie, brownie, and goblin brethren, the fey known as the Portunes were originally described by Gervase of Tilbury. According to Tilbury, Portunes were said to be quite tiny, less than half an inch high, with the weathered bodies and faces of elderly men. They lived peacefully alongside farmers and other laborers, invisibly helping with work and generally behaving benevolently. They had just one mischievous trait; on dark nights, if a Portune found a horseback rider traveling the moonlit roads alone, the Portune was rumored to invisibly join the rider, guiding the horse astray for miles before eventually leading it into a swamp. Once the horse and rider were good and stuck in the wetlands, the Portune would wander away, back to its home.[112]

The Boggart

One of the funniest stories in Keightley's book must surely be his account of a Yorkshire Boggart. The boggart, who was a pesky creature, moved uninvited into the home of a Yorkshire farmer. It tormented the whole family, especially the children, by stealing food and generally causing mayhem. Finally, the farmer's family was in such a state that he decided they needed to move. Together, the family packed up all their belongings, and just as they were leaving home, a neighbor stopped by to check on them. The neighbor asked if the family was moving away for good, and the farmer said that his

....

111. Keightley, *The Fairy Mythology*, 286.
112. Keightley, *The Fairy Mythology*, 285–86.

family had no choice but to flee. Just as the farmer finished speaking, a voice piped up from inside of some of the family's packed possessions. "Yes, yes, we're all fleeing!" It was the voice of the boggart.[113]

Changelings

To the parents of Britain, the creatures known as changelings must have been particularly terrifying. The fairies were rumored to be partial to stealing newborn babies and replacing them with changeling children. A changeling child would take on the appearance of the abducted baby it had replaced but often exhibited strange powers and supernatural precociousness. In one of Keightley's fairy stories, the mother of an abducted baby, desperate for the return of her own infant, tossed the changeling child onto an open fire. The screeching of the changeling summoned the fairies back, and they returned the woman's real baby in exchange for the changeling. Once the human baby was restored to its mother, the changeling child flew off into the night with its fey family.[114]

Cottingley Fairy Photographs

Though the famous Cottingley Fairy Photographs were taken after the end of the Victorian era, the story of the photographs captures the essence of the fairy craze that persisted throughout the Victorian era and into the 1920s. In 1917, in Cottingley, West Yorkshire, two young girls, Frances Griffiths (age nine) and Elsie Wright (age sixteen), told Elsie's parents that there were fairies in the garden of the Wright family cottage. When Elsie's parents didn't believe her, she borrowed her father's camera and inexplicably took a photo that appeared to show Frances with a group of fairies. Elsie's father

....

113. Keightley, *The Fairy Mythology*, 307–08.
114. Keightley, *The Fairy Mythology*, 355–56.

initially suspected that his daughter had tampered with the camera to produce the image, and he remained skeptical even after the girls took a second fairy photograph. However, in 1920, Elsie's mother attended a Theosophist lecture, and gave Elsie's photographs to the lecturer. Once the Theosophists had the photos, news of the Cottingley fairies spread throughout the Theosophist, spiritualist, and occult communities. A Theosophist named Edward Gardner came to Cottingley to investigate, and as part of his investigation, he asked Elsie and Frances to take more photos. To his excitement, the girls produced three more fairy photographs.[115]

Gardner decided that it was time to consult a specialist, so he invited a clairvoyant to Cottingley in August of 1921. Gardner wanted to see if the clairvoyant would corroborate the girls' story. The clairvoyant not only confirmed that the property was rife with fairy activity but also reported even more spirits than the girls had detected. In his notes, the clairvoyant logged sightings of an eight-inch-tall brownie, water nymphs and fairies, a golden fairy, a blue fairy, wood elves, a group of goblins, some gnomes, and handful of other assorted fey. Here is an excerpt from the clairvoyant's notes:

> **Fairy, Elves, Gnomes, and Brownie.** *(Sunday, August 14, 9 p.m. In the field.) Lovely still moonlight evening. The field appears to be densely populated with native spirits of various kinds—a brownie, fairies, elves, and gnomes.*
>
> **A Brownie.** *He is rather taller than the normal, say eight inches, dressed entirely in brown with facings of a darker shade, bag-shaped cap, almost conical, knee breeches, stockings, thin ankles, and large pointed feet—like gnomes' feet. He stands facing us, in no way afraid, perfectly friendly and much*

....
115. Silver, *Strange and Secret Peoples: Fairies and Victorian Consciousness*, 189–90.

interested; he gazes wide-eyed upon us with a curious expression as of dawning intellect. It is as if he were reaching after something just beyond his mental grasp. He looks behind him at a group of fairies who are approaching us and moves to one side as if to make way. His mental attitude is semi-dreamlike, as of a child who would say "I can stand and watch this all day without being tired." He clearly sees much of our auras and is strongly affected by our emanations.[116]

In the midst of the furor surrounding the photographs, Sir Arthur Conan Doyle, forever intrigued by all things supernatural, started writing about the Cottingley fairies. In 1922, he published a book about the photographs, *The Coming of the Fairies*, in which he argued that the fairies in the photos were real. Interestingly, in his introduction to the book, Doyle took pains to state that the legitimacy of spiritualism and the existence of fairies were entirely separate issues. He seemed concerned that people who found it hard to believe in the existence of fairies might sour on all supernatural phenomena, so he clarified that, to his mind, the existence of fairies and the existence of spirits after death were unrelated issues. So, just because someone was unconvinced by the fairy photographs didn't mean they had to doubt spiritualism too.[117] Doyle was very serious about spiritualism, and as a high-profile spiritualist, he didn't want his involvement in the hotly contested Cottingley affair to in any way tarnish spiritualism's reputation. Much later in life, long after Doyle's death, Frances would confess that all but one of the famous photos

116. Doyle, *The Coming of the Fairies*, 79.
117. Doyle, *The Coming of the Fairies*, 3–4.

had been tampered with. She maintained until her death that the last one was genuine.[118]

Floriography

In the Victorian era, many of the same feelings and fears that sparked a passion for fairies and folklore also led to a fascination with *floriography*, or the language of flowers. Various plants and flowers were ascribed specific meanings and could be used to communicate surprisingly detailed messages: confessions of love, expressions of grief, and declarations of intent. Perhaps the Victorians enjoyed the idea that savage jealousy, bitter regret, untamed passion, or unrequited infatuation might be hiding in plain sight, under the guise of a harmless flower arrangement; even the simplest bouquet could be evidence of a tawdry affair—or a broken heart.

Kate Greenaway's Language of Flowers

To give you a sense of the emotional intensity and specificity of the messages attached to many common herbs, flowers, and shrubs, I have included a selection of plants and their meanings. This selection comes from one of the great floral dictionaries of the Victorian era: *The Language of Flowers*, by British artist and author Kate Greenaway, published in 1884.

> *Aconite (Wolfsbane)—Misanthropy.*
> *Angelica—Inspiration.*
> *Aspen Tree—Lamentation.*
> *Asphodel—My regrets follow you to the grave.*
> *Belladonna—Silence*
> *Bluebell—Constancy.*

....
118. Silver, *Strange and Secret Peoples: Fairies and Victorian Consciousness*, 192.

Butterfly Weed—Let me go.
Carnation, Yellow—Disdain.
Chrysanthemum, Red—I love.
Chrysanthemum, White—Truth.
Chrysanthemum, Yellow—Slighted love.
Daffodil—Regard.
Dahlia—Instability.
Daisy—Innocence.
Dandelion—Rustic oracle.
Enchanter's Nightshade—Witchcraft. Sorcery.
Forget Me Not—True love. Forget me not.
Foxglove—Insincerity.
French Honeysuckle—Rustic beauty.
Geranium, Wild—Steadfast piety.
Harebell—Submission. Grief.
Hellebore—Scandal. Calumny.
Hemlock—You will be my death.
Henbane—Imperfection.
Hibiscus—Delicate beauty.
Holly—Foresight.
Hyacinth, White—Unobtrusive loveliness.
Hydrangea—A boaster. Heartlessness.
Iris—Message.
Jasmine—Amiability.
Lady's Slipper—Capricious Beauty. Win me and wear me.
Larkspur—Lightness. Levity.
Lavender—Distrust.
Lilac, Purple—First emotions of love.
Lilac, White—Youthful Innocence.
Lily, White—Purity. Sweetness.
Mandrake—Horror.

Marigold—Grief.

Mint—Virtue.

Mistletoe—I surmount difficulties.

Monkshood (Helmet Flower)—Chivalry. Knight-errantry.

Narcissus—Egotism.

Pansy—Thoughts.

Pennyroyal—Flee away.

Peony—Shame. Bashfulness.

Periwinkle, Blue—Early friendship.

Primrose—Early youth.

Rhododendron (Rosebay)—Danger. Beware.

Rose—Love.

Rose, White—I am worthy of you.

Rose, Yellow—Decrease of love. Jealously.

Rosemary—Remembrance.

Rue—Disdain.

Sage—Domestic virtue.

Snowdrop—Hope.

Sunflower, Tall—Haughtiness.

Tulip—Fame.

Valerian—An accommodating disposition.

Vervain—Enchantment.

Violet, Blue—Faithfulness.

Witch Hazel—A spell.

Wormwood—Absence.

Yew—Sorrow.[119]

....
119. Greenaway, *Language of Flowers*, 7–46.

Spring-Heeled Jack and Urban Folklore

Though the Victorians definitely had a passion and preference for the myths and legends of the countryside, with so many of them moving to cities, it was inevitable that superstitions, ghost sightings, and local lore would also spring up in these newer urban environments. As a result, in the nineteenth century, there were some notable scary stories and legends that were firmly rooted in modern urban life and featured the menacing Victorian cityscape as a backdrop.[120] These early urban legends provide a fascinating peek into the fears and anxieties that haunted the Victorian city.

One of the earliest and most famous Victorian urban legends is about the fiend known as *Spring-heeled Jack*. The first Spring-heeled Jack sighting was reported in 1837, the year Queen Victoria was crowned; Jack went on to be the terror of Victorian cities for roughly sixty years.[121] Between 1837 and 1904, Spring-heeled Jack was spotted in alleys and under bridges in cities all over the United Kingdom. No one could agree on who or what Spring-heeled Jack really was; sometimes he resembled a tall man in dark clothes, and sometimes he appeared in a much more monstrous form. Spring-heeled Jack could leap over walls and spring to the top of buildings in one leap (the move that earned him his moniker). He attacked people mercilessly and would menace anyone foolish enough to be walking alone at night, but he was thought to be particularly predatory toward women. According to some reports, Jack actually breathed blue flame on his victims.[122] Terrified witnesses who went to the press or the police with their Spring-heeled Jack sightings described him as

....

120. Mackley, "Spring-Heeled Jack: The Terror of London," 3, 11.
121. Mackley, "Spring-Heeled Jack: The Terror of London," 2.
122. Mackley, "Spring-Heeled Jack: The Terror of London," 12.

a devilish, demonic creature.[123] Though he hasn't been sighted since 1904, to this day, Jack remains one of the most iconic early urban legends.

Try It Yourself: Channel Your Inner Folklorist

You don't need a degree in folklore to record some local legends or note down some family tall tales. What stories matter to you? Which tales would you be sorry to see lost forever? We live at an odd time for preservation. On one hand, we are constantly reminded that "the internet is forever" and anything that we put online might one day return to haunt us. On the other hand, as more of our art, video, and writing exists only in digital format and not in hard copy, more and more of our creations are at risk of one day disappearing entirely. Don't assume that there's no value in the old ways, in bound books lined up next to each other on a shelf, in photographs framed on library walls, in stacks of old family journals preserved generation after generation.

So, try recording some of the stories that surround you. Remember that many of the world's most beloved folktales probably began as stories told to children at bedtime, rumors started by jealous neighbors, or legends that were invented to explain the strange aura of a place or person. Don't neglect the stories that might be very, very specific to where you live. Is there a joke told by residents of your apartment building about the strange noises that sometimes emanate from the boiler room? Does your college have an apocryphal tale of a freshman who disappeared under mysterious circumstances or a prank that got wildly out of hand?

If you have good relationships with older members of your family, you can ask them about anything strange they might have heard,

---

123. Mackley, "Spring-Heeled Jack: The Terror of London," 4.

but don't neglect the younger members of your family either. My advice? With the permission of their guardians, consult the children and teenagers you know. No one knows what might be hiding in the nearby woods better than a local four-year-old, and no one is more fascinated by urban legends of murder and mayhem than your thirteen-year-old goth cousin.

Old newspapers are also an excellent resource. If you can't access physical collections of old newspapers where you live, then see if you might have access to digital newspaper archives through a library membership or student ID. Many nineteenth-century newspapers have all kinds of stories about mysterious sightings, shocking coincidences, and improbable runs of bad luck. You might find the bones of a fascinating but long-forgotten regional legend if you dig around in the local archives long enough.

Writing is one way to preserve the anecdotes you uncover, but you could also record yourself or a friend telling the stories, as a DIY oral history project. If you're more inclined toward the visual arts, you can keep a sketchbook for drawing fey, nature spirits, and other creatures of the wild. The pages of your nature journal might fill with sketches of local creatures that you've heard stories of all your life, or you might decide for yourself the kinds of strange beings that stalk the local woods. Include some watercolor sketches of the famous local cryptid—or of the malignant spirit that keeps blowing out the pilot light of your water heater in the middle of winter. Jot some notes around the edges of your drawings, detailing the appearance, behavior, and nature of the creatures that surround your home.

Chapter 8
Fortune-Telling: A Subtle
and Stigmatized Craft

SERVANT GIRLS AND FORTUNE TELLERS.
At Newcastle, on Monday morning, Jane Gowdy, 64, was
charged as a rogue and a vagabond, and with having un-
lawfully professed to tell the fortune of one Jane Ramsay,
by means of cards, in the house No. 3, Marshall's Court,
on the 24th ult.
—From the pages of the *Manchester Courier*
and *Lancashire General Advertiser*, 1886[124]

The Victorian era was a confusing and even dangerous time to be a practitioner of the divinatory arts. The spread of spiritualism renewed public interest in fortune-telling, but old stigmas still clung to practices such as palmistry and cartomancy. While many spiritualists were fascinated by divination, fortune-telling for money was technically illegal throughout Britain and in parts of the United States; people who practiced divination professionally ran the risk of criminal prosecution.[125] In the public imagination, fortune-telling

....

124. "Servant Girls and Fortune Tellers," *Manchester Courier and Lancashire General Advertiser*, May 1, 1886.
125. McCrary, "Fortune Telling and American Religious Freedom," 272–73, 278.

was linked to the poor, criminals, and the uneducated (as well as to persecuted minority groups such as the Roma). Fortune-telling practitioners had a reputation as fraudsters, and their customers were often derided as gullible and unintelligent.[126] This stigma was a source of dismay to spiritualists who wanted to investigate the efficacy of cartomancy, palmistry, astrology, and crystal-gazing.[127]

Some Victorian spiritualists attempted to rehabilitate the image and reputation of fortune-telling. They tried to recast divinatory practices in a modern, scientific light, and they pushed to see them recognized as legitimate fields of inquiry.[128] The explosion of spiritualist and paranormal publications in the nineteenth century meant that there was a new way to disseminate divinatory advice, techniques, and troubleshooting. Spiritualist publications churned out articles tracking the movements of the stars, suggesting ways for readers to test their psychic abilities, and offering tips on scrying. Curious Victorians could peruse journals and periodicals for the most up-to-date advice on palmistry, crystal-gazing, and astrology.

But the nineteenth-century courts were definitely not on the fortune-tellers' side. Before the spiritualist craze started, the United Kingdom's Parliament had passed a law known as the Vagrancy Act of 1824. The Vagrancy Act was primarily intended to criminalize homelessness and begging; it meant that people sleeping outside, living in abandoned buildings, or asking for money could be prosecuted and punished. However, in addition to penalizing beggars and the homeless, the law was also intended to target anyone trying to earn money through the practice of the so-called subtle

....

126. "Prosecution of a Palmist," 185.
127. See "Prosecution of a Palmist," 185, and "The Cruelty of Superstition," 137–38, for spiritualist responses to the prosecution of fortune-tellers.
128. "Seeking Counsel of the Wise," 7–9
   "The Study of Psychical Phenomena," 24–26.

crafts, which the law defined as fortune-telling by palmistry or any other means.[129] The "subtle craft" provision haunted palmists, cartomancers, and astrologers for generations after the law's enactment. Meanwhile, across the pond, similar laws, modeled on the Vagrancy Act, popped up in states across the United States.[130] As a result, accepting money for divination was a risky game, and spiritualists who felt passionately about divination had to contend with centuries of stigmatization of the practice.

Nevertheless, despite the whiff of disrepute that clung to fortune-telling, there was plenty of interest in divination throughout the Victorian era. The Victorian sources consulted in this chapter include a mid-Victorian fortune-telling handbook, a multitude of instructional articles from the spiritualist journal *Borderland*, and a booklet of magical techniques written in 1906. Together, these texts paint a vivid picture of the fraught but fascinating world of fortune-telling in the nineteenth century.

Cartomancy

Cartomancy, or fortune-telling using a deck of cards, was a common Victorian divination practice. When the Victorians read the cards, they typically used a regular playing card deck rather than the tarot decks that are preferred by many cartomancers today. In the following pages, I have included a list of cards and their meanings from a popular 1861 fortune-telling handbook: *The Fortune-Teller; or, Peeps Into Futurity* by the Victorian writer Louisa Lawford. Lawford's method uses only thirty-two cards: the ace, king, queen, knave (a.k.a. Jack), ten, nine, eight, and seven of every suit. As you read through the meanings, you may notice that they are much less complex and

---

129. Vagrancy Act of 1824, Section 4, (1824).
130. McCrary, "Fortune Telling and American Religious Freedom," 272–73, 278.

much more unambiguously predictive than the meanings commonly attached to tarot cards today. While many modern cartomancers embrace layers of complexity, meaning, contradiction, and symbolism in their readings of various cards, the Victorians preferred straightforward predictions. They wanted simple foreknowledge of coming trials or triumphs in matters of love, money, and conflict. The deeper and more psychologically nuanced meanings that readers often use today are not part of Lawford's system.

The Fortune-Teller; or, Peeps Into Futurity

Ace of Clubs—Signifies joy, money, or good news; if reversed, the joy will be of brief duration.

King of Clubs—A frank, liberal man, fond of serving his friends; if reversed, he will meet with a disappointment.

Queen of Clubs—An affectionate woman, but quick-tempered and touchy; if reversed, jealous and malicious.

Knave of Clubs—A clever and enterprising young man; reversed, a harmless flirt and flatterer.

Ten of Clubs—Fortune, success, or grandeur; reversed, want of success in some small matter.

Nine of Clubs—Unexpected gain, or a legacy; reversed, some trifling present.

Eight of Clubs—A person's affections, which if returned will be the cause of great prosperity; reversed, those of a fool, and attendant unhappiness if reciprocated.

Seven of Clubs—A small sum of money, or unexpectedly recovered debt; reversed, a yet smaller amount.

Ace of Hearts—A love letter, or some pleasant news; reversed, a friend's visit.

King of Hearts—A fair liberal man; reversed, will meet with disappointment.

Queen of Hearts—A mild, amiable woman; reversed, has been crossed in love.

Knave of Hearts—A gay young bachelor, who dreams only of pleasure; reversed, a discontented military man.

Ten of Hearts—Happiness, triumph; if reversed, some slight anxiety.

Nine of Hearts—Joy, satisfaction, success; reversed, a passing chagrin.

Eight of Hearts—A person's affections; reversed, indifference on their part.

Seven of Hearts—Pleasant thoughts, tranquility; reversed, ennui, weariness.

Ace of Diamonds—A letter, soon to be received, and, if the card be reversed, containing bad news.

King of Diamonds—A man—generally in the army—but both cunning and dangerous; if reversed, a threatened danger, caused by machinations on his part.

Queen of Diamonds—An ill-bred, scandal-loving woman; if reversed, she is to be greatly feared.

Knave of Diamonds—A tale-bearing servant, or unfaithful friend; if reversed, will be the cause of mischief.

Ten of Diamonds—Journey, or change of residence; if reversed, it will not prove fortunate.

Nine of Diamonds—Annoyance, delay; if reversed, either a family or a love quarrel.

Eight of Diamonds—Lovemaking; if reversed, unsuccessful.

Seven of Diamonds—Satire, mockery; reversed, a foolish scandal.

Ace of Spades—Pleasure; reversed, grief, bad news.

King of Spades—The envious man, an enemy, or a dishonest lawyer, who is to be feared; reversed, impotent malice.

Queen of Spades—A widow; reversed, a dangerous and malicious woman.

Knave of Spades—An ill-bred young man; reversed, he is plotting some mischief.

Ten of Spades—Tears, a prison; reversed, brief affliction.

Nine of Spades—Tidings of a death; if reversed, it will be some near relative.

Eight of Spades—Approaching illness; reversed, a marriage broken off, or offer refused.

Seven of Spades—Slight annoyances; reversed, a foolish intrigue.[131]

Crystal-Gazing

Crystallomancy—the art of scrying with a crystal ball—was promoted by some Victorian occultists as a powerful psychic practice that could help budding clairvoyants discover and develop their abilities.[132] The indomitable Miss X (whom you may remember as one of the automatic writers introduced in chapter 3) was a passionate crystal-gazer, and her writing remains an excellent source of information on late Victorian crystallomancy. During Miss X's tenure as assistant editor of *Borderland*, she contributed quite a bit of advice on the theory and practice of crystallomancy. In one of her first

....
131. Lawford, *The Fortune-Teller*, 74–78
132. "The Art of Crystal-Gazing," 117, 119.

pieces for *Borderland*, she weighed in on the unfolding debate regarding the true source of messages received via crystal ball. The question was this: when a crystal-seer gazed into a ball and saw flashes of the past, future, or present, where were those images coming from? From the crystal-seer's unconscious? From their psychic powers? Or from some external source?[133] To Miss X's mind, there were at least three distinct possible sources, which she believed would produce the following three kinds of crystal visions:

1. Visions of things that were unconsciously observed by the crystal-seer but never penetrated their conscious mind. Miss X thought that crystal balls were uniquely effective at uncovering words, events, images, and scenes that people had encountered but not consciously registered. For example: if your eyes passed over a rack of newspapers while you were out running errands one day but you didn't stop to read any, then, according to Miss X, at your next crystal-gazing session, you might find images and headlines from those newspapers appearing in your crystal ball. Even though you had not paused to read the newspapers, and, if asked, you would have had absolutely no recollection of what was on them, Miss X believed that your mind could absorb the information and store it deep in your unconscious. She advocated for the use of the crystal ball to uncover such unconsciously absorbed information and bring it to the surface.

2. Images transferred from the minds of others to the mind of the crystal-seer via thought transference

....
133. "The Art of Crystal-Gazing," 119.

(which we now more commonly call telepathy). Miss X was fascinated by thought transference, which she experimented with using a multitude of techniques. According to her, the crystal ball was an ideal conduit for thoughts transmitted between people—either intentionally (as part of a deliberate experiment between two participants) or unconsciously and at random.

3. Visions of a potentially prophetic or clairvoyant nature. These were also said to be the least common kind of crystal vision; whenever a crystal-seer had a vision, it was much likelier to be an instance of thought transference or an unconscious observation rising to the surface of the mind.

Miss X also raised the possibility that the images glimpsed in crystal spheres were the work of spirits, but she seemed to consider it very unlikely.[134]

During its brief but lively run, *Borderland* published several beginner's guides to crystal-gazing. I have included a slightly modified version of these exercises under the "Try It Yourself" section at the end of this chapter.

Palmistry

Palmistry, also known as chiromancy, was widespread during the Victorian era, though public opinion of it varied enormously.[135] Many people viewed palmistry as little more than a fraud primarily

---

134. "The Art of Crystal Gazing," 119–21.
135. Joan Navarre, "Oscar Wilde, Edward Heron-Allen, and the Palmistry Craze of the 1880s," 174.

perpetrated by beggars and rogues; others considered it a pleasantly trivial parlor game for young ladies to entertain themselves with. However, curious spiritualists saw it as an ancient science ripe to be expanded upon and employed for modern purposes.[136]

Numerous chiromancy guides and instruction manuals were published, and *Borderland* even offered its readers opportunities to test their palmistry skills. The editor, W. T. Stead, would publish black and white photographs of hands, without supplying any information about the owner of the hands. Readers could then practice their palmistry on the photographed hands and try to work out what kind of person the hands might belong to. In a later issue, Stead would reveal the identity, profession, and other pertinent details of the person who contributed the photos so that aspiring palmists could judge how close to the mark their estimations had been.[137]

There was also an interesting debate about how palmistry really worked: whether it was "scientific" or "intuitive." Those on the scientific palmistry side believed that, fundamentally, palmistry was a science with set rules. In their view, certain lines on the hand corresponded to certain personality traits, and anyone could learn those correspondences and rules of interpretation from a palmistry handbook. However, people who believed in a more intuitive form of palmistry argued that the insights gleaned by palmists as they examined hands were only partly informed by a scientific reading of the lines of the hands; the rest of the information came from intuitive flashes that the palmist received from their contact with the hands. So, while part of an intuitive palmist's analysis would include a basic

....

136. "The Study of Palmistry," 75.
137. See again "The Study of Palmistry," 75–77. See also "Result of the Test Experiment in Reading Unknown Hands," 183–84.

interpretation of the lines of the hand, part of it would be more akin to a psychometric "reading" of the hand, fueled by the palmist's innate psychic ability. Those who categorized palmistry as an intuitive art pointed out that palmists occasionally intuited certain details for which there *were* no corresponding lines or marks in any of the published literature on palmistry.[138]

A Further Note on Phrenology and Palmistry

In both the introduction and the first chapter of this book, I alluded to the racism of phrenology and its relationship to eugenics. At this point, I'd like to flag for the reader that many Victorian palmistry handbooks also include at least passing mention of phrenology. Victorians who were interested in decoding the lines on people's palms were often also attracted to the tenets of phrenology, which posited that much about a person's morality, character, and intelligence could be determined from the shape, structure, and measurements of their head and face. Since interest in phrenology was widespread in Victorian Britain, there are unfortunately many references to it in nineteenth-century texts. I want to be upfront with my readers about the fact that anyone who goes looking for authentic Victorian palmistry texts is likely to also encounter phrenology handbooks and manuals.

During the Victorian era, practitioners of palmistry sometimes positioned palmistry and phrenology as sister sciences; however, they come from different roots and have separate histories. Palmistry is international and ancient. Some of the first mentions of palmistry in the Western world come from ancient Greece, thousands of years before the Victorians took up the practice.[139] Phrenology, on the

....

138. "Character Reading by Palmistry and Otherwise," 61.
139. Burnett, "The Earliest Chiromancy in the West," 189.

other hand, was developed by German and Austrian scientists in the early nineteenth century and was further popularized by British and American writers.[140] These were individuals operating within a colonial and imperialist framework, in societies that had a vested interest in arguing for the superiority of white people given the horrors they were visiting upon non-white nations and colonized peoples. So, while the Victorians may have seen palmistry and phrenology as equivalent practices, only one of them stemmed directly from a white imperialist framework bent on dehumanizing people of color.

Astrology

You might be surprised to find a section on astrology in a chapter about fortune-telling. Today, many astrologers would not necessarily choose to categorize astrology as a branch of fortune-telling; it's often seen as its own distinct practice. However, in the Victorian era, astrology was frequently grouped under the same umbrella as crystal-gazing, cartomancy, and palmistry. This was unfortunate for astrologers, because it left them vulnerable to arrest and prosecution under the same laws that ensnared cartomancers and palmists.[141]

Part of the trouble was that Victorian astrologers seem to have been rather rigidly predictive. Just like Victorian cartomancy was focused on foretelling specific, concrete events and outcomes, Victorian astrology was very oriented toward making definitive and ironclad predictions.[142] While modern astrologers tend to be more flexible in their interpretations of astrological charts, allowing room for various non-astrological factors and influences, Victorian astrologers were very dogmatic. They read personal horoscopes as desti-

---

140. Bryan C. Auday, "Phrenology," *Salem Press Encyclopedia of Health*, 2022.
141. Perkins, *The Reform of Time*, 57.
142. Perkins, *The Reform of Time*, 51–57.

nies set in stone, and they focused a lot of their energy on predicting exact timelines of events; they wanted to know when wars would start, when specific political figures would die, when the first freeze of winter would come, and so on.

Still, despite the rather inflexible nature of Victorian astrology, there must have been an enormous appetite for it. There was a proliferation of astrological books and periodicals, and occult societies, like the Hermetic Order of the Golden Dawn, that devoted themselves to studying the complexities and intricacies of the zodiac. Almost every issue of *Borderland* had a section devoted to astrology, which included everything from royal horoscopes (the charts of Queen Victoria's family members were sources of great interest!) to predictions of future economic and geopolitical events. There were even weather forecasts; astro-meteorology is not a very popular astrological subdiscipline in the age of televised weather forecasts and climate apps, but several issues of *Borderland* included contributions from astrologers who used the movement of the stars to make very specific weather forecasts months in advance. Of course, that was exactly the kind of behavior that could get an astrologer into trouble with the law.

One of the most famous British astrologers to find himself on the wrong side of the "subtle crafts" provision was a man named Alan Leo (1860–1917). During his prolific career as an astrologer, Leo founded multiple astrological societies, wrote a multitude of books on occult topics, and published an astrological magazine. Unfortunately, the British legal system didn't look kindly upon Leo's work, and he was brought up on criminal charges for fortune-telling several times. Even before his arrests, Leo had considered the astrology of his day too fatalistic and too focused on foretelling specific events. Leo wanted to redirect the focus of astrology toward the study of personalities, tendencies, and human character. He also hoped that shifting away from predictive astrology would allow astrologers to avoid the fortune-teller label. After his arrests, Leo began pushing for these changes in earnest; unfortunately, he died before he could see them take effect, but he has been called "the Father of Modern Astrology" because of his influence in steering the field toward its current incarnation.[143]

Astrology is a practice so ancient that it doesn't have one true form. Every generation alters it a little more, refashioning it for their age before handing it down to their children. Though our modern astrology is fundamentally different from the fortune-telling-by-the-stars practiced by the Victorians, there are still many striking similarities. For one thing, though we've largely abandoned astro-meteorology, we still have a taste for royal horoscopes!

Try It Yourself: Read the Cards

If you have experience with cartomancy, Louisa Lawford's 1861 card-reading system might be quite different from the one you use—so why not give it a try? Take a standard playing card deck and remove the twos, threes, fours, fives, and sixes of all four suits. Pick a question to ask the deck, and then draw as many cards as feels appropriate. Lay them out facedown, and then turn them over one by one, referring to the meanings provided in the cartomancy section of this chapter. Modern cartomancers sometimes advise that querants avoid yes/no questions and instead focus on complex and nuanced explorations of feelings, situations, and experiences. That's wonderful advice, but it's unlikely to be how many of Louisa Lawford's protégés would have practiced, so for this exercise, feel free to ask those straightforward questions about romance, career, and finances.

....

143. Patrick Curry, "Leo, Alan," *Oxford Dictionary of National Biography*, September 23, 2004, https://doi-org.stanford.idm.oclc.org/10.1093/ref:odnb/57150.

Try It Yourself: Practice Crystallomancy

The following exercise is a slightly condensed and modified version of a series of exercises promoted by *Borderland* as the ideal foundation for a beginner's crystal-gazing practice.

For crystal-gazing, any reflective object will do, but a glass or crystal ball is ideal; there's no need to be too picky as to the dimensions or quality of the crystal ball. After procuring a ball (or some other reflective item), position it so that it's not in direct light and is mostly shielded from reflecting any surrounding items. You don't want the crystal to be too bright or for the surface to be crowded with the reflection of nearby objects. You might position it so that part of it is shielded by a dark cloth. Of course, you will be able to see your own reflection as you gaze into the ball, but one way to handle that is to try to adjust your eyes' focus. Rather than focusing on the surface, where your reflection is visible, direct your gaze somewhere in the middle of the ball—this should reduce your awareness of your own reflection. It's also important not to strain your eyes. You can blink or glance away for a minute if you feel any discomfort.

Start your experiments with crystallomancy by setting aside ten minutes per day for a week to crystal-gaze. For the first five minutes of each session, don't try too hard to visualize anything, just let your eyes focus on the ball. For the next five minutes, try the following exercises:

1. Look at the room around you. Pick an object somewhere in the room, close your eyes, and try to visualize it with your mind's eye. Then, open your eyes, and see if you can visualize it in the depths of the crystal ball.

2. Next, close your eyes and visualize some simple scene from your recent memory—perhaps something that you experienced yesterday or the day before. Once you can picture the scene clearly, open your eyes and try to transfer it into the crystal ball. Practice this step over and over again, beginning with a simpler scene, and working your way up to a much more complex and active scene. For example, you might work your way up from visualizing your kitchen empty to visualizing your kitchen full of guests during a recent party.

3. Once you've mastered the first two steps, try visualizing a scene that you have recently read about or heard described to you. A scene from your favorite book would do nicely. Once again, begin by visualizing with your eyes closed, and then open them and transfer that vision to the crystal.

4. Next, try visualizing a scene entirely from your own imagination. Try to clarify all the details and colors with your mind's eye, then switch over to the crystal and try to envision it there.

5. Finally, go back to the beginning and work through exercises 1 through 4 again. However, this time you should try to cut out the initial visualization stage and go straight to the crystal ball without fixing the images in your mind's eye first.

You probably won't be able to work through all of these in just five minutes per day, so, when your time's up, finish whatever exercise you're on, and then pick up there the next day. Remember that you should always begin with five minutes of free crystal-gazing before five minutes of following the numbered exercises. Eventually, according to the Victorian crystal-seer who first devised this training practice, you should find yourself glimpsing interesting things in the crystal, even when you're not consciously trying to visualize them.[144]

....
144. "More about Crystal-Gazing," 529–30.

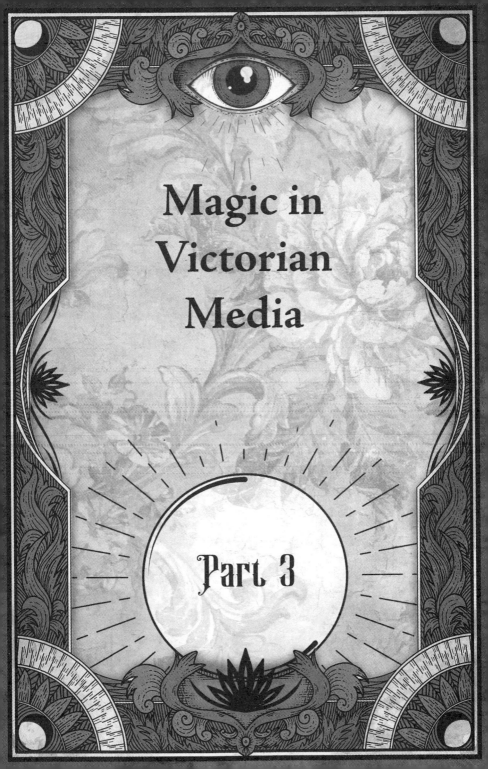

Magic in Victorian Media

Part 3

Chapter 9
The Victorian Gothic:
Literary Phenomena

*This was all so strange and uncanny that a dreadful fear
came upon me, and I was afraid to speak or move. The
time seemed interminable as we swept on our way, now in
almost complete darkness, for the rolling clouds obscured
the moon ... Suddenly, I became conscious of the fact that
the driver was in the act of pulling up the horses in the
courtyard of a vast ruined castle, from whose tall black
windows came no ray of light, and whose broken battle-
ments showed a jagged line against the moonlit sky.*

—Bram Stoker, Dracula[145]

The *gothic*. If there's one aesthetic that's instantly recognizable,
it's the gothic. You know it when you see it, and these days, you
see it a lot. Over the past two hundred and fifty years, the gothic has
worn many skins and spawned many subcultures, but it retains a
recognizable core that can be traced directly back to its roots in the
eighteenth century. While you might be surprised to find a chapter
on a literary genre in a book about Victorian magic and spiritualism,

....
145. Stoker, *Dracula*, 20.

the Victorian love of the gothic and the Victorian reverence for all things supernatural are twin echoes of the same song. Just as I would expect to find chapters about Greek mythology in a book about Hellenic magic, or sections about legend and folklore in a book on Celtic magic, I think of gothic tales as a key part of the Victorian supernatural landscape.

Early Gothic Fiction

Literary historians are generally in agreement that the gothic genre began with the publication of Horace Walpole's novel *The Castle of Otranto* in 1764, a full seventy-plus years before Queen Victoria ascended the throne. In the seven decades between *The Castle of Otranto* and the beginning of Victoria's reign, there was a positive deluge of pre-Victorian gothic fiction published in Britain. There are two major sub-types of the early gothic novel: the *explained* and the *unexplained* supernatural.

In the explained supernatural, the protagonist (often an innocent young woman fallen on hard times and preyed upon by some malevolent man) experiences all manner of seemingly supernatural phenomena, which, by the end of the novel, turn out to have a rational, non-paranormal explanation. Usually, one of the novel's villains has been up to no good, and the heroine has been misled by the events she witnessed—either because the villain deliberately intended to trick her or because she got carried away in her terror. A modern, more humorous equivalent of the explained supernatural would be the original episodes of the animated series *Scooby-Doo*, in which the seemingly supernatural trouble is usually caused by human criminality instead. Mysterious lights on the swamp late at night belong to smugglers, or a disgruntled heir is dressing up as a ghost to scare his cousins so that he can sell the family estate. One way or another, the seemingly supernatural events are explained. Some classic pre-Victorian examples of the explained supernatural are the novels of Ann Radcliffe, one of the most famous and influential early gothic novelists.

In the unexplained supernatural, the terrifying occurrences turn out to be genuinely supernatural phenomena. These stories tend to end on a darker and more violent note. One notorious example of the unexplained supernatural, *Vathek*, written by William Beckford and published in 1786, contains a series of intensely violent episodes and then ends with the main character literally descending to hell to experience eternal damnation.

The Victorian Gothic

The division of the gothic into the explained and unexplained supernatural is mostly an artifact of the pre-Victorian gothic novel—the gothic novel of the eighteenth and very early nineteenth century. The Victorian era was the heyday of the ghost story, and many of the most popular Victorian gothic novels were definitively supernatural. The Victorians adored ghosts and other supernatural entities and were passionately fanciful—they preferred not to have supernatural events explained away.[146]

Gothic Heroines

The gothic novel isn't something that the Victorians invented—it's something they inherited, modified, and arguably even perfected. So, just what was at the core of the Victorian gothic novel? Its heroines, for one thing. The gothic is a genre that is deeply concerned with gender and has been since its inception. Many of the great early gothic novelists were women, such as Ann Radcliffe and Eliza Parsons, and many of the most influential gothic novels feature innocent

....
146. Briggs, "The Ghost Story," 177.

young heroines who must be defended—or defend themselves— against all manner of devilry and debauchery. Some excellent examples of this are Jane Eyre from Charlotte Brontë's 1847 novel *Jane Eyre*, Mina Murray from Bram Stoker's *Dracula* (1897), and Laura from Sheridan Le Fanu's *Carmilla* (1872).

Gothic heroines are often sensitive, highly intelligent, and very perceptive; they see things that others don't, whether of natural or supernatural origin. They also tend to display a great deal of moral courage. When faced with what is easy or what is right, they usually choose to do the right thing, no matter how terrifying the consequences might be. In gothic heroines, you can see the foremothers of the modern-day so-called final girls of horror films. The heroine might occasionally be rescued by another character or by a fortuitous turn of events, but often she must rely on her own intelligence, resourcefulness, and inner strength. The gothic heroine may be menaced by a supernatural force, like a family curse, or by a gothic villain. The gothic villain is often, but not always, an older male figure who seeks to marry, kill, rape, imprison, or steal the fortune of the gothic heroine.

The gender dynamics of the gothic were not set in stone, however. As the gothic genre matured, it became increasingly likely to distort or subvert its own tropes. Sheridan Le Fanu's villainess Carmilla is an excellent example of the subversion of the trope of the gothic villain. Carmilla seems like a young and innocent maiden, but she is an ancient vampire with sexual and maybe murderous designs on the novella's sweet and shy heroine, Laura. In another reversal of typical gender dynamics, in the beginning of *Dracula*, Jonathan Harker finds himself in a situation that would be relatable to many a gothic heroine: imprisoned in a forbidding Eastern European castle by an older man with mysterious and menacing intentions.

Gothic Protagonist as Spiritualist Medium

Whether the protagonist of a Victorian gothic novel is male or female, it is very common for the main character to be the first (or only) character to realize that something is seriously wrong. Many of these protagonists seem to have an almost superhuman ability to perceive things that are not obvious to other people. Many of them are ghost-seers, people who unexpectedly encounter ghosts invisible to everyone else around them (for more information on the difference between a medium and a ghost-seer, see chapter 6).

In fact, fictional gothic protagonists shared many qualities with professional mediums—particularly their capacity to walk in the shadowy borderland between seen and unseen, living and dead, mystery and revelation. Throughout its long history, from the novels of Radcliffe to the films of Jordan Peele, the gothic has given voice to the voiceless and expression to the suppressed. In their own way, spiritualists often attempted to do the same, whether by channeling the spirit of a murder victim or speaking out in support of abolition and suffrage. Spiritualists also tended to present themselves as morally and religiously motivated, just as gothic protagonists were often written as pious and upstanding.

The Cursed Family and the Haunted Home

The power (for good or for ill) of family, lineage, and inheritance was at the heart of the Victorian gothic. At its roots, the Gothic is about being endangered in the very place you should feel safest: at home, in your own household. Many of the most popular gothic plots hinge on something cursing, haunting, hunting, corrupting, or possessing a family (or family home). The gothic abounds with family curses, buried injustice, domestic violence, and murderous ancestors. It makes sense that these themes would have struck a particularly powerful chord with the Victorians, who had a fixation on the familial and the domestic. While much of their popular culture focused on praising and propping up the middle-class family, that image of a safe, cozy, and loving household had a shadowy twin in the gothic, which painted vivid pictures of the dangers that could lurk at home. Beautiful young women could be visited by vampires in their beds. Children could be possessed by the malignant ghosts of their ancestors. Dark family secrets, long buried, could burst forth in the form of spirits seeking vengeance.

The gothic villain (or villainess) often embodies the threat of the past erupting violently into the present. Perhaps the villain murdered someone many years ago, and their castle is now haunted by their victim's ghost. Perhaps they are an immortal supernatural creature, a vampire or succubus born in a different age, with a century's worth of blood on their hands. Perhaps they keep their first wife trapped or imprisoned somewhere, and the strange cries that the heroine keeps hearing are screams for help. In the gothic, the phenomena and strange occurrences witnessed by the protagonist are often manifestations of some old evil that must be exposed and then laid to rest.

For spiritualists, the haunted house was also a key lodestone. The very first spiritualist séances took place in a family home reportedly haunted by the ghost of a murder victim (for more information on the investigations at the Fox family farmhouse, see chapter 5). Throughout the spiritualist era, amateur investigators were encouraged to experiment at home with séances and other forms of spirit communication. Though there were plenty of public spiritualist performances and lectures, spiritualism's foundation was domestic—the haunted household transported from the page into reality.

Gothic Phenomena

Phenomena are key when we think about the potent link between spiritualism and the gothic. One of the hallmarks of gothic fiction is the presence of phenomena: strange sights, sounds, or other occurrences that make the protagonist doubt their own senses and understanding of the world around them. The sound of a child's laugh in a supposedly empty house. A glimpse of a shadowy figure in the window of a boarded-up attic. A persistent feeling of being watched. An instant in which a corpse seems to move or make a sound. Phenomena are important to the gothic because they are frightening and build tension but also because the gothic can be a deeply psychological genre, and phenomena can make us doubt ourselves and disbelieve our eyes and ears.

By spiritualism's zenith in the nineteenth century, phenomena were no longer limited to fictional tales of the unearthly. Spiritualists were deeply committed to recording, researching, and investigating the phenomena that they themselves had witnessed—during séances and otherwise. Those gothic whispers and shadowy figures had slipped out of the library and into the Victorian drawing room, where they were obsessively documented and studied by devoted investigators.

Science, Medicine, and Psychology

Mad scientists. Bubbling vats of poison. Horrifying medical procedures. Organs suspended in glass jars. Taxidermy. Autopsy. Blood transfusions. Grave robbery. Mental asylums. All these figures, themes, and settings seem quite at home in the gothic genre now, but they weren't integral to the gothic originally, not in the eighteenth century. It was the Victorians, following in the footsteps of the inimitable Mary Shelley, who added a generous helping of weird science and macabre medicine to the gothic.[147]

Forensic Science

There are many ways to talk to the dead. While Victorian spiritualists were delving into the mysteries of spirit communication, some investigators, of a very different kind, were developing their own techniques for decoding messages from the deceased. From the mid-nineteenth century through the early twentieth century, police detectives and criminal investigators began experimenting with many new methods, including fingerprinting, ballistics, and criminal profiling.[148] The chapter on Victorian paranormal investigations has more detailed information about the evolution of policing and investigation during the Victorian period; for the purposes of this chapter, it's just important to note that as criminal investigation techniques became increasingly complex and elaborate, gothic fiction became more and more saturated with forensic methods and medical or scientific investigators. One intriguing and well-known example is Bram Stoker's famous vampire hunter Van Helsing, who uses his scientific background to profile, track, and fight Dracula.

Macabre Medicine

The Victorians had lots of reasons to be anxious about doctors. For one thing, Victorian doctors were not always that good at their job. In addition to their infamous penchant for bloodletting, or *bleeding* patients who were sick, they also lacked our modern understanding of germs and so practiced astonishingly poor hygiene for much of the nineteenth century. In fact, it wasn't until the 1840s that

....

147. Arntfield, *Gothic Forensics*, 6–8.
148. Arntfield, *Gothic Forensics*, 8.

someone first suggested that it might be a good idea for doctors to wash their hands in between autopsying a corpse and delivering a baby.[149] At the time, it was standard practice for doctors at a hospital to go straight from handling dead (and often diseased) cadavers to treating patients, without any hygiene practices in between. So, until doctors developed a better understanding of germs and cleanliness, they were quite literally taking disease with them everywhere they went, and specifically from the dead to the living.

Then there were the cadavers themselves, which were also a point of contention. In the nineteenth century, as now, medical students needed to work with cadavers as part of their training, but by the 1820s, the demand for bodies far outstripped the supply.[150] Since legally obtained cadavers were difficult to come by, the illegal trade in corpses flourished and thrived. Unscrupulous individuals known colloquially as resurrectionists would rob graves and sell the bodies to doctors and medical students (who knew better than to ask questions).[151] Mary Shelley's *Frankenstein* is a fascinating and famous example of the literary fixation on the trope of the grave robber, body snatcher, or resurrectionist.

This body shortage crisis led the United Kingdom Parliament to pass a new law, the Anatomy Act of 1832, which increased the number of bodies that medical students were allowed to dissect.[152] The Anatomy Act permitted the dissection of any donated body. However, since the Victorians were largely horrified by dissection, autopsy, and the more macabre side of medical research, there weren't many people willing to sign up to donate their own body after death.

....

149. Aptowicz, *Dr. Mütter's Marvels*, 256–58.
150. Montgomery, "Resurrection Times," 539.
151. Montgomery, "Resurrection Times," 534.
152. Montgomery, "Resurrection Times," 542.

Instead, most of the "donated" cadavers were the unclaimed bodies of people who had died in prisons, hospitals, and workhouses: in short, they were usually the bodies of very poor people.[153] The Victorian poor were outraged by the Anatomy Act, which they felt stripped them of their right to a respectful Christian burial after death. It also meant that the very poor, the people who were the least likely to be able to afford the services of a doctor or to receive prompt medical attention, were the ones whose bodies would be used against their will after their death to further medical advances that would largely benefit the wealthy and middle class.

All of this, the disease, the bloodletting, and the body snatching, clung to the Victorian-era doctor like the stench of the grave, so it is hardly surprising that frightening doctors and morbid medicine became such key tropes in the Victorian gothic. This pervasive anxiety about doctors might also speak to why psychic doctors and trance healers became so popular in the nineteenth century. Unlike traditional physicians, spiritualist doctors didn't buy bodies or carve up cadavers. While conventional doctors were associated with robbed graves and rotting flesh, spiritualist physicians worked with the spirits of the dead (not their bodies) and practiced a cleaner, less morbid kind of healing.

The Threat of the Asylum

In the nineteenth century, the threat of institutionalization loomed over the lives of Victorian women. It was alarmingly easy for men in Britain and America to have their wives and other female relatives involuntarily committed to mental asylums. Any form of independence, defiance, or even the mildest symptoms of mental illness

....
153. Montgomery, "Resurrection Times," 542.

could be used as justification for institutionalization.[154] Even before the Victorian era, the gothic genre had explored the ways women were confined by society (and especially trapped by male relatives and other authority figures). The Victorian gothic novel took the already long-standing trope of the innocent young woman taken captive against her will and compounded it by adding the threat of lifelong imprisonment in a mental hospital. The figure of the psychologist, psychiatrist, or asylum doctor also became increasingly important (and threatening) in gothic fiction over the course of the nineteenth century.

Taken together, it makes sense that physicians, forensic scientists, and psychiatrists took on a ghoulish hue to the Victorian reading public. Like the spiritualists who sought to penetrate the veil between worlds, these scientists also walked in the dim borderland between life and death—and often their path was much gorier and more bloodstained. The macabre nature of their professions, as well as the terrifying power they wielded over society's most marginalized, earned them a powerful role in the Victorian gothic.

Major Gothic Novels and Novellas

I have included Mary Shelley's *Frankenstein* in the list below because even though it predates Victoria's reign by about two decades, it altered the gothic genre forever. Mary Shelley initiated the fusion of science, medicine, and the gothic, and you'll find her fingerprints on the gothic, horror, and science fiction genres to this day.

+ *Frankenstein* (1818) by Mary Shelley
+ *Wuthering Heights* (1847) by Emily Brontë

....
154. Kate Moore, "Declared Insane for Speaking Up," *Time*.

- *Jane Eyre* (1847) by Charlotte Brontë
- *Carmilla* (1872) by Sheridan Le Fanu
- *Strange Case of Dr. Jekyll and Mr. Hyde* (1886) by Robert Louis Stevenson
- *The Picture of Dorian Gray* (1891) by Oscar Wilde
- *Dracula* (1897) by Bram Stoker
- *The Turn of the Screw* (1898) by Henry James

Try It Yourself: Explore Your Own Shadow

If the gothic is anything, it is a conduit for creative expression. The gothic offers the opportunity to investigate the shadows of our world, to touch darkness and confront death. Try your hand at creating your own gothic piece of writing or art. You don't need to stick to the tropes and traditions of the Victorian gothic. The gothic is a way to experience and play with the things that terrify us—the fears that shadow us during our waking hours and stalk us in our dreams. What frightens you most? Is there a way to explore it creatively? Even if you don't consider yourself an artist or a writer, you might find it valuable to experiment with some form of gothic expression in any medium. In fact, the gothic is a startlingly multimedia genre and subculture by nature. Many gothic enthusiasts express themselves not just through music, painting, and writing, but also through interior design, fashion, jewelry making, and other art forms.

Try It Yourself: Read a Gothic Tale

You've read *about* the gothic, now it's time for you to read the gothic! The gothic genre is now so well established that readers are spoiled for choices. If you want to read something more recent, something from the twentieth century or later, then your options are too numerous to list;

the gothic has exploded into a plethora of different styles and subgenres. If you want to understand the roots of the genre, you can venture even further back than the Victorian era and read some eighteenth-century gothic novels. Ann Radcliffe's *The Mysteries of Udolpho* (1794) is not only a classic—it's arguably the archetypical gothic novel. Eliza Parsons's *The Castle of Wolfenbach* (1793) is also an excellent introduction to the first golden age of the gothic novel.

I've already listed some of the classics of the Victorian gothic earlier in this chapter. If you decide to read a tale of terror from the Victorian era, then, while you read, devote some time to considering what it was like to read these stories during the nineteenth century, when spiritualism was at the height of its popularity. It must have been remarkable to sit by the fire on a winter's night and read tales of ghosts in an age when spirit communication was a common practice and many people, from average everyday folk to some of the leading figures of the day, were personally experimenting with mediumship and séances.

Chapter 10
Pre-Raphaelite Art:
Seers and Sorceresses

She left the web, she left the loom
She made three paces thro' the room
She saw the water-flower bloom,
She saw the helmet and the plume,
She look'd down to Camelot.
Out flew the web and floated wide;
The mirror crack'd from side to side;
'The curse is come upon me,' cried
The Lady of Shalott.
—ALFRED, LORD TENNYSON,
"THE LADY OF SHALOTT"[155]

Circe Invidiosa—the jealous enchantress goddess of ancient Aeaea. *Miranda*—Shakespearean heroine, castaway on an enchanted isle with her wizard father and a host of unearthly creatures. *Cassandra*—Princess of Troy, cursed by the god Apollo to see the future but to never be believed. These women of myth and legend were the muses of the Pre-Raphaelite painters of Victorian Britain.

---

155. Tennyson, *Poems*, 15.

In modern New Age and goddess-worshipping communities, the Pre-Raphaelites still have an enthusiastic following thanks to their commitment to depicting magic, witchcraft, enchantment, and the divine feminine. If you recognize the iconic painting of Ophelia, ill-fated lover of Hamlet, submerged in a river with just her face and hands above the water, then you've glimpsed the work of John Everett Millais, one of the founders of the Pre-Raphaelite Brotherhood. If you've seen the lush depiction of an auburn-haired Lady of Shalott, clad in a white dress and seated in a boat richly draped in fabrics, then you've also encountered the art of John William Waterhouse.

Who Were the Pre-Raphaelites?

Though many different artists and writers later came to be affiliated with the Pre-Raphaelites, the Pre-Raphaelite movement officially began in London in 1848 when seven painters, poets, and critics banded together and declared themselves the Pre-Raphaelite Brotherhood (or PRB for short).[156] The seven original members included the artists William Holman Hunt, John Everett Millais, and Dante Gabriel Rossetti.[157] They called themselves the Pre-Raphaelites because they saw themselves as channeling the artistic practice of an earlier, purer time, a time that predated even the Renaissance master Raphael. They didn't mesh well with some of the leading artists of their day, and they founded the Brotherhood to define and promote their own distinctive art theory and style. Though the official Brotherhood only lasted about five years before it broke up, various artists

....

156. Robinson, *The Pre-Raphaelites*, 14.
157. Malcolm Warner, "Millais, Sir John Everett, first baronet (1829–1896), painter," *Oxford Dictionary of National Biography*, September 23, 2004, https://doi-org.stanford.idm.oclc.org/10.1093/ref:odnb/18713.

were loosely associated with the movement for decades afterward.[158] Pre-Raphaelite art is not always given its due in art history books, but no exploration of the status of myth, legend, and mysticism in the Victorian era would be complete without a nod to the Pre-Raphaelites and their work.

Where Were the Witches?

The cultural figure of the witch was in a complicated transitional state during the Victorian era. The infamous witch trials of earlier centuries were well in the past, but the birth of Wicca was years in the future. Witches were no longer quite the stock villain characters that they had once been, but they also weren't widely seen as sympathetic figures or as the protagonists of their own stories.[159] While magic and mysticism were alive and well during the Victorian era, nineteenth-century occult practitioners, spiritualist investigators, and mediums avoided terms like *witch* and took pains to distance themselves from anything that might have been viewed as satanic or malicious.[160] Even in fiction, witches were not as common as they are now—they appeared periodically, but they were massively outnumbered by the hordes of ghosts that drifted through Victorian popular fiction.

But on the canvases of the Pre-Raphaelites, the sorceresses and enchantresses of earlier ages lived on. Circe. Medea. Morgan le Fey. La belle dame sans merci. The Pre-Raphaelites gave faces to the witches, seers, and sirens of antiquity.

....

158. Robinson, *The Pre-Raphaelites*, 237.
159. For more on the evolution of witches as protagonists and heroines over the course of the nineteenth century, see: Ronald Hutton, "Witches and Cunning Folk in British Literature 1800–1940," *Preternature: Critical and Historical Studies on the Preternatural* 7, no. 1 (2018): 37.
160. Oppenheim, *The Other World*, 65–67.

The Pre-Raphaelites and Medievalism

The Pre-Raphaelites were at the forefront of Victorian medievalism, the nineteenth-century enchantment with the history and legends of early Britain (medievalism is explored in greater detail in chapter 7).[161] Rather than charging forward into a new age with masculinized depictions of emerging science, technology, and urban centers, the Pre-Raphaelites looked back to a time of ancient temples, crumbling castles, and swaths of untamed wilderness. They didn't typically paint crowded scenes reminiscent of the hustle and bustle of the Victorian city center. Instead, they often focused on depicting just a few people, or even a solitary figure, captured in a moment of reverie, reflection, or great emotion.

Pre-Raphaelite art is very interested in materiality; the Pre-Raphaelites weren't stingy with details. They loved clothes and props and paid special attention to every fold of fabric, every thread of embroidery, every lustrous pearl and sparkling ring. Their paintings entice the viewer into the canvas and into luxurious, sparkling, shadowy worlds of swaying tapestries and dusky rose gardens and billowing gowns. They were world builders, offering a fantasy of long ago and far away to Victorians, who felt rushed and harried by the commotion of modern life.

The Divine Feminine

The Pre-Raphaelites were also very open-minded in their choice of subjects. Their art venerated Pagan witches and pious biblical figures alike. Their vision of divinity was not limited to Christianity and often favored the women of myth over the characters in the Bible. This is interesting because there was a lot of confusion about women,

....
161. Lepine, "The Pre-Raphaelites," 488.

magic, and divinity in the Victorian era. Since the Victorians revered the domestic and the familial, they liked to think of women as inherently nurturing, gentle, maternal, and pious creatures; women were characterized as having a certain innate sacred power within the home.[162] This marked a shift from earlier ages, when women were often characterized as inherently more lustful, degraded, debauched, and degenerate than their much holier male counterparts. In many respects, this shift was an improvement. As feminine intuition and powers of perception were recast in a more positive and less demonic light, the threat of witch hunts or persecution (the bane of the seventeenth-century midwife or cunning woman) was reduced.[163]

But the Victorian elevation of women to domestic angels came with strings attached. To retain their status, women had to adhere to a stifling and repressive code of conduct. As the scholar Vanessa D. Dickerson argues in her book *Victorian Ghosts in the Noontide*, it was all very well for women to minister as domestic angels within the home, but once they stepped out of it and tried to use their gifts in the public sphere, Victorian society quickly became uncomfortable and ambivalent. As a result, the women who came forward and decided to utilize their intuition and other "feminine powers" in order to work as mediums and psychics occupied a complicated place in society. Such women had to chart an incredibly narrow course between the judgments and expectations of society and their own desires and abilities.[164]

The Pre-Raphaelite's vision of women was also conflicted. Their era was full of seers and mystics. If they wanted to paint a woman in a trance or a woman in a magic circle, they didn't need to venture

....

162. Dickerson, *Victorian Ghosts in the Noontide*, 29.
163. Hutton, "Witches and Cunning Folk in British Literature 1800–940," 44.
164. Dickerson, *Victorian Ghosts in the Noontide*, 28–31.

back to the shores of ancient Greece or Rome. They could have wandered down to one of the local performance halls to see any one of many mediums perform. But the Pre-Raphaelites largely rejected the seers of their own age—perhaps because they saw them as tawdry: too modern in their techniques and too commercialized. They eschewed the professional, middle-class, working mediums of the nineteenth century and instead offered a vision of women's innate magic that was mythologized and unattainable: archaic, divine, and lost to the erosion of time.

However, while the Pre-Raphaelites may have avoided painting the working mediums and psychics of their own time, their classical and medieval subjects included murderesses, adulteresses, and, of course, witches. On one hand, the Pre-Raphaelites painted a picture of womanhood that was heavily romanticized and unattainable for mere mortals. On the other hand, the very characters they romanticized were transgressive, violent, powerful, and defiant.

Pre-Raphaelite Subjects

Who were the characters that so captivated the Pre-Raphaelites? We don't have room in this book to study every goddess or siren that materialized on Pre-Raphaelite canvases, but I've picked four of my favorites for this chapter: the Lady of Shalott, Ophelia, Circe, and Medea. Together, the stories of these women touch on most of the themes and tragedies that colored the Pre-Raphaelite imagination.

Arthurian Ladies and Renaissance Maidens: Ophelia and the Lady of Shalott

Over the centuries, the Lady of Shalott has appeared in many tales under many names, but the heart of her story—her tragic death—rarely changes. The story of the doomed noblewoman and her ill-fated love for Lancelot dates to at least the thirteenth century, but it was popularized again in the nineteenth century by Alfred, Lord Tennyson.[165] Tennyson was poet laureate of the United Kingdom from 1850 to 1892, enjoyed renown as the most celebrated poet of his era, and is still considered the premier Victorian poet today.[166] Like the Pre-Raphaelites, Tennyson was chasing the past for much of his career. He wholeheartedly embraced medievalism, and many of his most successful poems were based on Arthurian legend, though classical figures, such as Ulysses, appear in his poetry as well. Tennyson reintroduced the Lady of Shalott to the Victorians and, in doing so, added a layer of enchantment to her tale. His poem "The Lady of Shalott" is stunningly visual and depicts the Lady as an artistic enchantress who watches the world through her mirror and spins visions on her loom.

In Tennyson's poem, the Lady of Shalott is already cursed from the poem's first lines. She is doomed to die if she leaves her tower or even tries to look out the window. Rather than risk death, she gazes into a mirror pointed at the window and watches reflections of the world outside of her tower. Eventually, however, she sees Sir Lancelot of Camelot riding by. Overcome by her desire for him, she glances away from her mirror and looks directly at the window. In doing so, she triggers the curse, but she is also finally able to leave her tower and venture outside. She goes down to the banks of the river, climbs into a boat, and floats down the water to Camelot as she dies:

> *With a steady stony glance—*
> *Like some bold seer in a trance,*

....

165. Levine, "Tirra-Lirrical Ballads," 439.
166. Christopher Ricks, "Tennyson, Alfred, first Baron Tennyson (1809–1892), poet," *Oxford Dictionary of National Biography*, September 23, 2004, https://doi-org.laneproxy.stanford.edu/10.1093/ref:odnb/27137.

Beholding all his own mischance,
Mute, with a glassy countenance—
She look'd down to Camelot.
It was the closing of the day:
She loos'd the chain, and down she lay;
The broad stream bore her far away,
The Lady of Shalott.
As when to sailors while they roam,
By creeks and outfalls far from home,
Rising and dropping with the foam,
From dying swans wild warblings come,
Blown shoreward; so to Camelot
Still as the boathead wound along
The willowy hills and fields among,
They heard her chanting her deathsong,
The Lady of Shalott.
A longdrawn carol, mournful, holy,
She chanted loudly, chanted lowly,
Till her eyes were darken'd wholly,
And her smooth face sharpen'd slowly,
Turn'd to tower'd Camelot:
For ere she reach'd upon the tide
The first house by the water-side,
Singing in her song she died,
The Lady of Shalott.[167]

It makes sense that Tennyson's Lady captured the Pre-Raphaelite imagination. She has all the hallmarks of the figures who fascinated them: a legendary backstory, an association with magic and

----

167. Tennyson, *Poems*, 17–18.

witchcraft, and a fate at once tragic and romantic. She was also symbolic of Victorian women more generally; the sphere of acceptable options and opportunities for Victorian women could be depressingly narrow, as narrow as the tower that confines the Lady of Shalott. So many women were claustrophobically limited to the domestic sphere, discouraged—or even forbidden—from venturing beyond the roles of wife and mother. So, the symbolism of the Lady getting up from her loom, walking across the room, and freeing herself from her prison by dooming herself to die must have been especially powerful during the Victorian era.

It's not a coincidence that two of the most famous Pre-Raphaelite paintings are Waterhouse's depiction of the Lady of Shalott and Millais's painting of Ophelia. Both women are ensnared by ill-fated romance. Both women defy the restrictions of their station and circumstances but ultimately succumb to tragic fates. At the beginning of *Hamlet*, Ophelia appears a sweet and demure maiden, but after mounting tragedies drive her to madness, she becomes difficult, unpredictable, and lewd. Ophelia's demise is left somewhat ambiguous in Shakespeare's play, but it is likely a death by suicide. For Ophelia, like the Lady of Shalott, the price of rebellion is death.

Magic and Monsters: Circe and Medea

If the Pre-Raphaelites were fascinated by women and tragedy, they were also fascinated by women and power. Two particularly potent women who frequently appear in Pre-Raphaelite art are the ancient sorceresses Circe and Medea. In contrast to the more delicate ladies of Arthurian legend, the Circe of Greek myth is a powerful, vengeful enchantress. She turns men into animals, takes lovers, and rules over her own island as something halfway between queen and goddess. Circe is best known for her appearance in Homer's *Odyssey*. After Odysseus and his men land on Circe's shores, she promptly prepares a glorious but tainted feast for them. Odysseus' men eat and are immediately turned into swine. The Pre-Raphaelites were clearly intrigued by Circe, given how frequently they painted her. Unlike the ideal woman as envisioned by Victorian society (reassuringly wifely, maternal, and pious), Circe is sly, passionate, powerful, and subordinate to no one.

Medea is another witch of antiquity who found her way onto Pre-Raphaelite canvases. Her story is one of horror, revenge, and the most unforgivable of all crimes. Medea is the daughter of a king and the descendant of the sun god Hyperion. Most significantly, she is also a priestess or dedicant of the witch goddess Hekate. Medea appears in many myths, but she is probably best known for her story as it is told by the great Greek tragedian Euripides. In Euripides's play, Medea and her two sons are cast aside by Medea's husband, Jason, who wants to be rid of his first wife so that he can marry a young princess. Savage in her drive for revenge, Medea gifts the princess with a cursed dress that poisons the young woman. Then, in the ultimate act of vengeance, Medea murders her two sons by Jason, determined to make him feel the same pain that she does. Like Circe, Medea uses supernatural powers and all manner of herbs and potions to bend the world to her will. Both women cause havoc and distress for the men who dare to cross them. And, unlike the doomed Ophelia and Lady of Shalott, both women live on, unpunished for their various transgressions against society. Significantly, the Pre-Raphaelites didn't paint these women as hideous, leering monsters but rather as captivating, thoughtful, and often beautiful enigmas.

Taken together, the characters that the Pre-Raphaelites found most fascinating were a contradictory group. These characters are at turns powerful, passionate, vengeful, doomed, defiant, tragic, triumphant—some of them resigned to their unfortunate destiny, others fighting it until their last breath. The Victorians loved these romanticized women of myth and legend, but they were also frightened by their power and transgressive nature. There is also an echo of the spiritualist woman's dilemma in these stories: the woman who sees all but is never believed; the woman who dooms herself by freeing herself; the woman who seizes power, but at a terrible price.

Pre-Raphaelite Painters

There were many artists associated with the Pre-Raphaelite movement over the course of the nineteenth century, but I've chosen to highlight four that might be of particular interest to readers of this book.

Dante Gabriel Rossetti (1828–1882)

The Byronic libertine of the Pre-Raphaelite art movement, Dante Gabriel Rossetti was notorious for his numerous affairs and bohemian lifestyle. Born in Britain, but Italian by descent, Rossetti distinguished himself as a poet and a painter; he was also the brother of Christina Rossetti, a notable Victorian poet who composed the brilliant "Goblin Market." The hair and faces of Rossetti's portraits are highly distinctive and easily recognizable; he had a strong preference for red-headed models with striking profiles. Rossetti was an obsessive and eccentric artist with a habit of becoming romantically involved with his models.[168] He was married to the most well-known Pre-Raphaelite model, Elizabeth Siddal (who modeled for Millais's *Ophelia* and was also an artist in her own right), but it was

....

168. J. B. Bullen, "Rossetti, Dante Gabriel (1828–1882), painter and poet," *Oxford Dictionary of National Biography*, September 23, 2004, https://doi-org.stanford .idm.oclc.org/10.1093/ref:odnb/24140.

a turbulent union, and he engaged in a series of affairs. Rossetti's works of interest include *Proserpine, Joan of Arc*, and *Lady Lilith*.

John Everett Millais (1829–1896)

As a founding member of the Pre-Raphaelite Brotherhood and the artist behind the most iconic Pre-Raphaelite painting, *Ophelia*, John Everett Millais was at the heart of the Pre-Raphaelite movement. As a boy, Millais showed artistic promise early, and he was considered something of a prodigy before he began to rebel against the academic painting style that was the prevailing mode at the time.[169] His co-founding of the Pre-Raphaelite Brotherhood in 1848 was nothing short of an artistic scandal.[170]

Unlike some of his more disreputable peers, such as the infamous Rossetti, Millais at least tried to avoid impropriety in his personal life, but he was at the center of a scandal in the 1850s when Effie Gray, the wife of the esteemed art critic John Ruskin, left her long-unconsummated marriage to Ruskin to marry Millais.[171] Gray's disastrous marriage with Ruskin and her ensuing romance with Millais has been the source of rumors and speculation for the past 160 years, and it's also the subject of several books and films.

In addition to *Ophelia*, a few of Millais's paintings that might particularly interest readers of this book include *The Martyr of Solway, The Grey Lady*, and *Mariana*. Millais also delved into a historical murder mystery with his 1878 painting *The Two Princes Edward and Richard in the Tower*, which is an artistic depiction of the two

....

169. Malcolm Warner, "Millais, Sir John Everett, first baronet (1829–1896), painter," *Oxford Dictionary of National Biography*, September 23, 2004, https://doi-org.stanford.idm.oclc.org/10.1093/ref:odnb/18713.

170. Robinson, *The Pre-Raphaelites*, 16.

171. Robinson, *The Pre-Raphaelites*, 21–22.

fifteenth-century child princes, who vanished mysteriously from the Tower of London in 1483 and are believed to have been murdered.

John William Waterhouse (1849–1917)

Merely an infant when the PRB was originally founded, John William Waterhouse later came to be associated with the final generation of Pre-Raphaelite painters in the late 1800s. Waterhouse was trained in art at the Royal Academy Schools, and he eventually became well known for his paintings of magical and mythical women.[172] Though he was one of the last Pre-Raphaelite painters, his paintings of legendary and literary figures are some of the most enduring works produced by the movement. Waterhouse was particularly intrigued by Circe—he depicted her in his paintings *Circe Offering the Cup to Odysseus*, *Circe Invidiosa*, and both of his versions of *The Sorceress*. Other fascinating paintings by Waterhouse include *Hylas and the Nymphs*, *The Lady of Shalott*, *Miranda*, *The Magic Circle*, and *Lamia*.

Evelyn De Morgan (1855–1919)

Born to a wealthy family in 1855, Evelyn De Morgan (née Mary Evelyn Pickering) enjoyed a rich and varied education, including the study of Greek and Latin, extensive travel, and early exposure to Renaissance art. De Morgan's passion for painting emerged in her childhood, and the intensity of her obsession dismayed her family, who saw it as inappropriate for a girl. Nevertheless, De Morgan was relentless in her pursuit of artistic training and practice, and her family reluctantly allowed her to enroll in the Slade School of Fine

....

172. Peter Trippi, "Waterhouse, John William (1849–1917), figure painter," *Oxford Dictionary of National Biography*, September 23, 2004, https://doi-org.laneproxy.stanford.edu/10.1093/ref:odnb/38885.

Art (one of the only art schools that accepted female pupils) when she was seventeen.[173] De Morgan practiced intensively and channeled her early exposure to classical mythology into stunningly executed paintings of classical subjects.

She married William De Morgan, a potter, in 1887, and she and her husband devoted their lives to artistic, activist, and spiritual pursuits; the De Morgans were pacifists, spiritualists, and supporters of the women's suffrage movement.[174] De Morgan and her husband were regular practitioners of automatic writing, and her spiritualist and occultist bent is evident in much of her work, including her paintings *Cassandra*, *Medea*, *The Love Potion*, *The Storm Spirits*, and *Daughters of the Mist*.[175]

Try It Yourself: Pathwork with the Pre-Raphaelites

The meaning of the term *pathworking* has shifted over the years. Llewellyn's online encyclopedia describes pathworking as "originally the process of astrally or mentally projecting up and around the paths of the Kabalistic Tree of Life in order to gain information, instructions, meet entities there, and ask favors of those entities. More recently, some popular writers have described any visualized journey as pathworking, and this has become the popular meaning of the term."[176] In this exercise, I use the term *pathworking* in its more general sense, to refer to a directed visual meditation. You will use the combined powers of your imagination, concentration, and in-

....

173. Smith, "The Art of Evelyn De Morgan," 3–4.
174. Rachel S. Gear, "Morgan, (Mary) Evelyn De [née Mary Evelyn Pickering] (1855–1919), painter," *Oxford Dictionary of National Biography*, September 23, 2004, https://doi-org.laneproxy.stanford.edu/10.1093/ref:odnb/45491.
175. Smith, "The Art of Evelyn De Morgan," 6.
176. "Pathworking," The Llewellyn Encyclopedia, Llewellyn, accessed November 29, 2022. https://www.llewellyn.com/encyclopedia/term/pathworking.

tention to voyage into the mythic realm of the Pre-Raphaelites. You may script out a journey in advance, planning a voyage that includes specific characters and experiences, or let the visualization unfold more spontaneously.

Many people who base their pathworking on a piece of art use tarot or oracle cards. They pick a specific card with artwork they find especially meaningful, and then they project themselves into the card through sustained meditation. Pre-Raphaelite art can have a very tarot-like energy since the paintings often center on mythical characters or medieval royalty. However, since Pre-Raphaelite paintings usually have extremely rich, decorative, and evocative backgrounds and are much larger than a tarot card, they contain more details than most tarot cards have room for. Those detailed backgrounds make the paintings ideal for immersive pathworking.

Pick a piece of Pre-Raphaelite art that you find particularly potent. If you're not an enormous fan of the Pre-Raphaelites, then you can always search for some more modern Pre-Raphaelite-inspired art. You could also work backward and find some earlier art with similarly mythic and magical subjects. When you pick your painting, try to choose a piece that seems to really reach out to you and beckon you into its frame. Have you ever stared at a painting and wanted to slip inside of it? That's exactly the feeling you're trying to cultivate with this exercise.

You should also consider how you feel about any figures in the painting. Do the characters speak to you in some way? The Pre-Raphaelites painted a lot of people adrift in reverie, but they also painted figures experiencing moments of heightened emotional intensity. You might pick your piece according to its emotional valence. Perhaps the character in the painting looks the way you feel or is portrayed at a crucial moment that you can relate to given current events in your own life.

Be sure to think deeply about your relationship to the painting before you start working with it. What draws you to this particular painting? Ask yourself what you want out of this visualization. Do you want a fantastical escape from your own life? A chance to ask Circe for power or Cassandra for vision? Do you want to walk the walls of ancient Troy or ride with the Valkyrie? Determine whether you want to script out your journey into the artwork or just explore the world freely. If you want to script your journey in advance, you can write a guided meditation for yourself, record yourself reading the script, and then play it as you meditate.

Scripted or unscripted, you may begin by taking a comfortable seated position in front of an image of the painting. This could just be your laptop screen with the artwork visible, or you could print out a copy of the painting and stick it on your wall. It may help to dim the lights slightly, although not so much that you can't see the painting. Breathe evenly and try to release distracting thoughts and images. Focus on the painting. Many people pathwork with their eyes open, but you can also try closing your eyes if that's more comfortable.

Imagine the painting as a doorway that you can walk or climb through. If you've scripted and recorded a guided meditation to accompany this visualization, you can start playing the recording at this point and follow along. Otherwise, you can just follow your intuition. When it feels right, imagine yourself entering the world of the painting through the frame. Once you're on the other side of the painting, you should be able to turn your head and view more of the world than was visible in the original image. There also may be places and characters beyond the original scope of the painting that you wish to visit.

For example, if you used one of my favorite Waterhouse paintings, *Miranda* (the 1916 version), for pathworking, then once you entered the painting, you might find yourself on a rocky and wind-swept coastline, standing just behind Shakespeare's heroine, Miranda, as she watches a distant shipwreck. You might hear the cries of seabirds and perhaps even screams from the distant, doomed ship. You might stand on the coastline with Miranda to ask her questions or just experience the world of the painting. But, if you know something about Shakespeare's play *The Tempest*, you also might turn and strike out for the island's interior to speak to Miranda's sorcerer father, Prospero. You might ask Prospero for advice or power or interact with the world of *The Tempest* in some other way.

Whatever your aims, you can use the focused meditation of pathworking to encounter these characters in their own mythological landscape, to ask them for strength or wisdom, to understand them on a deeper level, and to gain insight into your own psyche and life's path. When you're ready to leave the world of the image, you can walk back to the place you entered, exit the painting, and leave the meditative state.

Once you're finished, reflect on your experience. Don't be hard on yourself if you had trouble with the exercise—this level of extended visualization is not easy and takes some practice for most people. If you want to try again, you can keep returning to the same painting, or you can experiment with other pieces of artwork. Try to keep some record of your pathworking journey, perhaps in a journal or by recording yourself describing the experience.

If you are visually impaired or find sustained creative visualization difficult or unappealing, you might try working with a literary source instead. For example, you might select one of Tennyson's poems and write yourself into it, scripting your journey through the landscape with your words rather than with your mind's eye. You can describe yourself walking up to the Lady of Shalott's tower or taking a seat next to her on her voyage to Camelot. As with all the creative exercises in this book, the point of this experiment is to flex some creative muscle and see what your mind can do, so don't feel restricted or like you must do the exercise exactly "by the book."

Try It Yourself: Create Like a Pre-Raphaelite

For many readers of this book, the preoccupations of the Pre-Raphaelites are probably quite familiar. Like many of us, they were drawn to the romances, tragedies, and deities of old. For this exercise, you can slip on Pre-Raphaelite lenses and work on your own creative interpretation of a mythological, biblical, legendary, or literary subject.

Choose a character that feels particularly powerful and resonant for you personally. If you love classical mythology and Arthurian legend, then you might pick a classically Pre-Raphaelite subject, such as Morgan le Fey or Circe. But you can also make a more unconventional or modern choice, such as a character from one of your favorite films. What matters most is that you pick a figure who has archetypical, personal, or spiritual significance for you. In whatever medium you feel most comfortable, create a piece of art that depicts, honors, or explores the character you've chosen. If you aren't particularly proficient or interested in the visual arts, then you can certainly find another way to connect with the character. The Pre-Raphaelites were an extremely literary group; many of them were writers as well as artists, and they were closely affiliated with some of the top poets of their day. Rather than sitting down with a paintbrush, you might try writing a poem or a song or even a fragment of highly descriptive prose.

You can go more abstract if you want, but the Pre-Raphaelites were great lovers of detail, so the more you can anchor your work with important symbols and objects that allude to specific features of the character's story, the better. If you're painting Persephone, you might try to include a pomegranate. If you're writing about Circe, you might include mention of the sailors-turned-swine that roam her island.

You can also put a doubly Victorian spin on this exercise and choose to paint or write about a Victorian spiritualist, medium, or clairvoyant. You can pick one of the spiritualists discussed in this book or do your own research and find another figure that inspires you. Once you've chosen someone, you can give them the Pre-Raphaelite treatment, whether with easel and canvas or pen and ink.

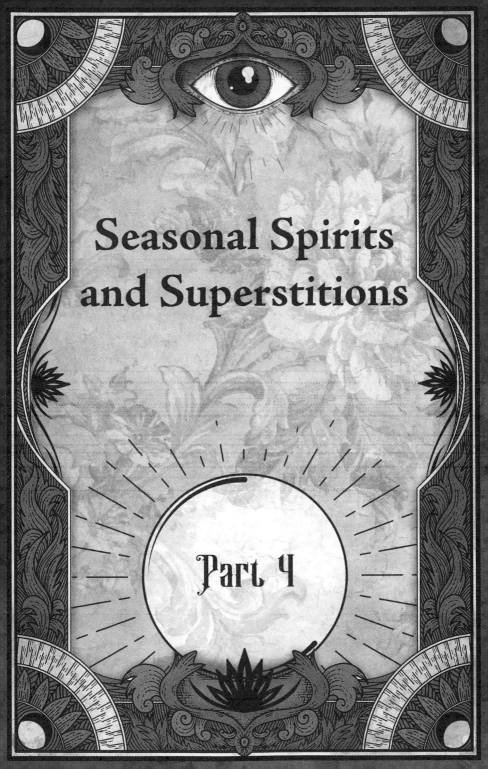

Seasonal Spirits and Superstitions

Part 4

Chapter 11
Hallowe'en Celebrations:
Ghosts, Goblins, and Grooms

Popular superstition has given the thirty-first day of October a peculiar character of its own, no other day of the year having so many and such strange customs attached to it. Witches, devils, fairies and disembodied spirits walk abroad on that night; charms and divinations attain their highest success with all and any who wish to try them.
—THE LADIES' HOME JOURNAL, OCTOBER 1892[177]

I t's a breezy autumn night in 1897. Guests gather in the parlor for a dance, wearing their most outlandish costumes, and enjoy an array of fruits, nuts, and candies. The hostess's three children appear in an elaborate *tableau vivant*, dressed as goblins and brownies. As the hour grows late, the children are sent to bed, and the adults indulge in fortune-telling games, predicting all manner of romance and mischief for the year ahead. Welcome to a Victorian Hallowe'en party!

....
177. "Superstitions of Halloween," *Ladies' Home Journal*, October 1892.

Chapter 11

The History of Hallowe'en

The celebration we currently call "Halloween" comes from a mix of ancient Celtic religion, old Christian customs, and Irish and Scottish immigrant traditions. In this chapter, we're taking a closer look at Hallowe'en traditions (specifically in North America) from about 1830 to 1920. Where did they come from, what were they all about, and how can you celebrate Hallowe'en like it's 1897? One of this chapter's primary sources is a book published in 1919: *The Book of Hallowe'en* by American writer and librarian Ruth Edna Kelley. Kelley was one of the first to attempt a comprehensive history of Hallowe'en, and her book is a valuable compendium of vintage Hallowe'en celebrations and lore.

As for the origin of Hallowe'en, what we know for sure is that our modern celebration is a direct descendant of the early Christian holy day All Hallows' Day, which was also known as All Saints' Day. All Hallows' Day, which was celebrated on November 1, was a religious holiday devoted to praying for the souls of Christian saints and martyrs. The day after All Hallows' Day, November 2, was known as All Souls' Day and was intended for prayers for the souls of all departed Christians. The night before All Hallows' Day was All Hallows' Eve, which fell on October 31. Together, All Hallows' Eve, All Hallows' Day, and All Souls' Day make up a triduum (a three-day religious holiday) known as Allhallowtide.

For many medieval Christians, Allhallowtide was when they would pray for their dead relatives to be released from purgatory and allowed into heaven. Purgatory is a less popular concept now than it once was, but for centuries it was a cornerstone of Christianity: an unpleasant halfway house where souls would go when they hadn't quite earned a spot in either heaven or hell. Their living relatives could offer up prayers in hopes of freeing them from purgatory and ushering them into heaven. The more prayers that were sincerely offered on behalf of a soul, the likelier that soul was to escape purgatory. Thus, for much of England's history, it was customary for the poor to go from door to door during Allhallowtide, offering to pray for the souls of the dead. The rich would then offer the poor food in return for promises to pray for the dead relatives of the wealthy.[178] Different as that may sound from our modern Hallowe'en, you can catch echoes of it in our twenty-first-century celebrations. Strangers going door to door. Treats given to garner good will. Food and celebrations but with the backdrop of the restless dead and souls in pain.

It is also commonly suggested that Hallowe'en's roots stretch back even further than the Christian church. Some theorize that the church may have chosen the date of All Hallows' Day to coincide with a Pagan celebration that occurred around the same time of year.[179] The Celtic name for this celebration was Samhain. Samhain fell about halfway between the autumn equinox and the winter solstice and marked the coming of winter. It was also supposed to be a time of heightened supernatural power: all manner of fey, demons, and spirits were alleged to be more active (and thus more likely to interfere in human affairs) on Samhain.[180] When they arrived in the United States, Scottish and Irish immigrants brought this complicated mix of old Celtic folklore and early Christian superstition. Ultimately, this tangle of Pagan and Christian practices evolved into the festival we now know as Hallowe'en.

....
178. Kelley, *The Book of Hallowe'en*, 98.
179. Kelley, *The Book of Hallowe'en*, 29.
180. Kelley, *The Book of Hallowe'en*, 16–22.

The Spirit of Hallowe'en

It's important to remember that to nineteenth-century celebrants, Hallowe'en was really about mischief, horror, and mystery of a specifically *supernatural* nature. Modern Hallowe'en stories and media include plenty of non-supernatural slashers, serial killers, and sadists. These figures and tropes are more recent additions to the season. For the Victorians, the supernatural element was key. Witches, specters, black cats, and bats were significant Hallowe'en motifs, and so were diminutive fey like fairies, goblins, and brownies. Maniacal human killers and extreme human-on-human violence were not usually part of nineteenth-century Hallowe'en lore. To the extent that Hallowe'en was associated with human crime, it was usually of the petty or mischievous variety, not the truly gory. The Victorians were more likely to envision a troop of Hallowe'en fairies frolicking through their moonlit garden than to imagine a knife-wielding psychopath paying their neighborhood a visit. So, if you're trying to channel your inner Victorian this Hallowe'en, you'll want to lean more heavily on supernatural tropes and figures, ranging from mischievous sprites and brownies to witches and ghosts, rather than axe murderers and serial killers.

Romance and Fortune-Telling

For the nineteenth-century Americans who enthusiastically celebrated the nation's spookiest holiday, the night of Hallowe'en had a certain romantic appeal—quite literally. It was believed to be the best night of the year for fortune-telling, especially divination related to romantic and marital prospects.[181] There was a whole host of techniques recommended for young single people curious—or

....

181. Arkins, *Halloween*, 13.

nervous—about the identity of their future spouses. The "Try It Yourself" section at the end of this chapter includes one of my favorites: a classic Hallowe'en midnight scrying exercise.

It is interesting that a holiday known for its ghosts and goblins was also closely associated with marriage, love, and romance. In the nineteenth century, marriage was a serious matter, and the stakes were particularly high for women. Women had limited options outside of marriage, so they were expected to make husband-hunting a priority. Unfortunately, since divorce was much less accessible than it is now, it wasn't easy for Victorians to get out of a marriage gone bad. Young people who made the wrong choice would likely live with the repercussions for the rest of their lives. The consequences could be particularly severe for women, who were often very dependent, both financially and legally, upon their husbands.

Given the high stakes, it makes sense that women might have sought supernatural guidance on the most bewitching night of the year.

Hallowe'en Parties

In some respects, nineteenth-century Hallowe'en parties were a lot like ours. Hosts decorated their houses, guests were instructed to wear costumes, and the night was all about sweets and treats. However, since Victorian hosts didn't have the same access to factory-made costumes and props that we do (and certainly didn't have the option of switching on a scary movie if people got bored!), they had to be particularly inventive.

Here are a few of the tricks nineteenth-century hosts kept up their sleeves. These lively anecdotes and suggestions come from the pages of turn-of-the-century women's magazines, which published fun and creative tips for Hallowe'en parties every autumn.

✦ Hallowe'en party invitations were themselves an opportunity for creativity and whimsy. Some hosts instructed their guests to keep the invitation a secret, just to add to its air of mystery and mischief. One contributor to *Ladies' Home Journal* in the autumn of 1902 described the tradition like this:

In getting up a Hallowe'en party make everything as secret and mysterious as possible and the greater will be the fun. I had the good fortune, many years ago, to be bidden to such a frolic. My card of invitation was decorated with water-color drawings of bats, owls, black cats and witches' brooms, surrounding the following snatch of doggerel: "Come at the witching hour of eight, and let the fairies read your fate; reveal to none this secret plot, or woe—not luck—will be your lot."[182]

✦ Since nuts were an important Hallowe'en treat, they were often part of the night's trickery. One inventive hostess carefully sliced open a handful of walnuts, removed the kernels, and filled the empty nuts with little treats like tiny dolls, brass rings, and small carvings. She then glued the walnuts halves back together and mixed them into a bowl of perfectly normal walnuts. At dinner, the guests were provided with a nutcracker and the bowl of nuts—apparently, there was quite a stir when they began cracking their walnuts and discovered that some of them contained surprises![183]

....

182. "A Jolly Hallowe'en Party," *Ladies' Home Journal*, October 1902.
183. "For Halloween," *Good Housekeeping*, October 1904.

✦ Long before we had plastic pumpkins to carry our candy in, the Victorians were using real pumpkins to store their treats. *Ladies' Home Journal* offered the following instructions on creating a fruit centerpiece in the year 1900:

Select a golden-colored, medium-sized, well-shaped pumpkin. With a sharp knife, fashion it into the form of a basket with an old-fashioned tub handle on each side. Carefully scoop out the seeds and pulp, leaving a thin shell. Polish the rind and fill the basket with apples, pears and grapes of various tints.[184]

✦ In ancient Greek mythology, the Fates were three goddesses responsible for the fortunes of all mortals. Since fortune-telling was such an important part of Hallowe'en in the nineteenth century, the Fates were popular symbolic figures on Hallowe'en night. Some parties included people dressed up as the three Fates, and some hosts liked to send their guests home with little fortunes (sort of like the ones that we pull out of fortune-cookies today). One magazine suggested that hosts dress up as the Fates and give out fortune cards with random lines of poetry on them. These cards would be handed to the guests as they left the party, and it would be up to each guest to decide how to interpret the poetic message on their fortune card.[185]

....

184. "Hallowe'en or Harvest Dishes," *Ladies' Home Journal*, November 1900.
185. "Old and New for Halloween," *Good Housekeeping*, October 1892.

Chapter 11

Hallowe'en and Spiritualism

Interestingly, I haven't found evidence that Hallowe'en was a day of particular significance to nineteenth-century spiritualists. If they held special Hallowe'en séances, or took the day seriously at all, then the evidence is not in any of the archival collections I've searched. Perhaps spiritualists didn't want to make a connection between Hallowe'en and their own faith because Hallowe'en was widely associated with tricks, mischief, misbehavior, and superstition. This was essentially the opposite of the reputation that serious spiritualists were trying to cultivate; they wanted their practice to be seen as reverent, religious, and scientific.

Try It Yourself

Since nineteenth-century Hallowe'en celebrations varied widely from region to region, there are many different traditions and customs to try if you want to celebrate your own Victorian-flavored Hallowe'en. The following are just a few fun suggestions, drawn from women's magazines and Kelley's Hallowe'en book.

Make a Hallowe'en Card

If you're into Hallowe'en imagery, then you've almost certainly seen them: lively, imaginative, eccentric Hallowe'en postcards from the turn of the century. Overflowing with pumpkins, witches, bats, and cats, these iconic cards offer a colorful glimpse of the Hallowe'en celebrations of long ago. Postcards became very popular in the late nineteenth century and went on to enjoy a heyday, known as the golden age of postcards, from the 1890s to about 1920. During those years, postcards were all the rage, and every holiday offered an excuse for people to send a flurry of postcards to their friends and relatives.[186] Hallowe'en cards were very popular and sometimes doubled as invitations to Hallowe'en parties or dances. Unfortunately, Hallowe'en cards fell out of fashion after the golden age of postcards ended, and they are now much less common than Christmas or birthday cards.

If you want to enjoy an old-fashioned Hallowe'en celebration, why not start by making some Hallowe'en cards to send to your friends? If you're planning to throw a Hallowe'en party, your cards might double as invitations. You can look up old images of Victorian cards for inspiration. Lots of early Hallowe'en cards featured rhymes or snippets of poetry, so you might try making up your own spooky rhyme or quote a few lines of poetry by someone like Edgar Allan Poe.

Note: I would be remiss if I didn't flag for readers the racist nature of some of the imagery used on Hallowe'en cards at the turn of the century. While many of the Hallowe'en postcards we've inherited from that time are harmless fun, some include racist caricatures. The deep shadows of the past have a lot to teach us about our own faults and failings now, in the twenty-first century. We can't change what was put on a postcard in 1898, but we can learn from past cruelty and make the decision not to include racist imagery and appropriation in our modern Hallowe'en celebrations.

Stage a Hallowe'en Tableau Vivant

Tableau vivant is French for "living picture." A tableau vivant is an immersive art form halfway between a painting and a theatrical performance. People decorate a space, set up a scene, don costumes, strike poses, and then freeze to create a flesh-and-blood picture for the amusement of their friends. Tableaux vivants became popular at

....
186. Arkins, *Halloween*, 15.

the end of the eighteenth century, were a common party game and source of entertainment throughout the nineteenth century, and then fell out of favor in the twentieth century.[187]

The Victorians used tableaux vivants to depict specific scenes from history, myth, literature, or art. One source from 1902 describes an especially lively Hallowe'en party that included three tableaux vivants. The first depicted a scene from Shakespeare's play *Macbeth*: the three witches hunched over their cauldron, chanting. The second tableau was another Shakespearean scene: Hamlet with his father's ghost. For the third tableau, the hostess herself was reportedly suspended from the ceiling on a broomstick (apparently there was some apparatus holding her aloft that was concealed behind a curtain—what a remarkable sight she must have been!).[188]

There are many reasons why tableaux were popular for so long: they're social, creative, can be extremely festive, and give everyone an opportunity to dress in costumes. Staging tableaux might be the perfect Hallowe'en activity; there's lots of fun to be had by turning your living space into a seasonal scene and then stepping into the frame. So, how do you go about staging a Hallowe'en tableau vivant? First, find some friends to join you. You can certainly do a tableau alone, but a lot of the fun is the teamwork. Next, pick a scene to depict. It could be something very literary, like a moment from *Macbeth*, *Dracula*, or *Frankenstein*, but you could also try something more modern, like a tableau of a scene from *Beetlejuice* or *Hocus Pocus*.

Next, select costumes and décor and decide who will portray which character. Where will each person stand, and what will their pose be? You also need to pick a place to stage your tableau. Since tableaux vivants were originally parlor games, a living room would

....
187. Jacobs, *Framing Pictures*, 90–93.
188. "A Jolly Hallowe'en Party," *Ladies' Home Journal*, October 1902.

do quite nicely. Decorate the space you've chosen to match the scene you're staging. Indulge your creative side, but don't break the bank either; there's no need to be as over-the-top as the hostess suspended from her ceiling on a broom! Most Victorians just made the best of whatever room they had. Once the scene is decorated and the actors are dressed, everyone can grab their props, head for their spot in the tableau, and strike their pose.

Scry with an Apple and Mirror Divination

Apples have had various supernatural and mythological associations throughout history, and in the Victorian era, they were popular tools for harvest season fortune-telling. Nineteenth-century Hallowe'en lore includes a dizzying array of divination methods featuring apples. Since Hallowe'en was a time for romantic and marital scrying, many of these practices were intended to help young single people (especially women) catch a glimpse of their future spouse. Here is one of my personal favorites from Kelley's book:

> *A Hallowe'en mirror is made by the rays of the moon shining into a looking-glass. If a girl goes secretly into a room at midnight between October and November, sits down at the mirror, and cuts an apple into nine slices, holding each on the point of a knife before she eats it, she may see in the moonlit glass the image of her lover looking over her left shoulder, and asking for the last piece of apple.*[189]

Since it's not 1892 and we're not all eagerly awaiting a peek of our future husband, this can certainly be adjusted to accommodate those who have no interest in scrying for a partner. Decide which

189. Kelley, *The Book of Hallowe'en*, 78.

aspect of your future you want to scry for: do you want a preview of your home, career, or family a few years down the road? As the sun sets on Hallowe'en, place a mirror somewhere you'll be undisturbed—preferably across from a window with a view of the moon. Keep the room dimly lit (candlelit is best). As the hour approaches midnight, select an apple and a knife, and sit down at the mirror. Watch yourself in the glass as you cut the apple into nine slices and consume them one by one. Right before you eat the final slice, look at the space behind your left shoulder in your reflection. Whom or what do you see?

Chapter 12
Christmas Ghost Stories:
The Spirits of Midwinter

*What could have been more appropriate for the telling
of tales of spectres and the sheeted dead, for the thrilling
of nerves and the creeping of flesh, than a Christmas Eve
or the night of Christmas Day itself, in the days gone by,
when hall and cottage held hospitable revel?*
— FROM THE *LIVERPOOL MERCURY*,
DECEMBER 25, 1894[190]

The children are up past their bedtime, sitting on the knees of
their aunts, uncles, and grandparents, bellies full after the best
dinner they've had all year. It's Christmas Eve, one of the longest
nights of the year, and the wind is cold enough to bring tears to the
eye, but everyone is inside, wrapped in shawls, fortified by warm
drinks, and gathered around the fireplace. Grandfather stokes the
flames in the hearth as one of the aunts begins to speak. She tells a
story as old as any hand-me-down or heirloom in the house, a story
that has been passed down generation after generation. It is a story

---

190. "Christmas Ghosts," *Liverpool Mercury*, December 25, 1894.

about family, about home and hearth and the shadows that linger there. It is a story about ghosts.

By the mid-nineteenth century, the Victorian passion for ghost stories was burning brightly, and the genre had its own season: the Christmas season. Guests at holiday parties challenged each other to see who could come up with the most chilling tale. Periodicals released at Christmas time published eerie tales of hauntings and apparitions. Popular authors such as Charles Dickens released frightening new stories every year. If Christmas was in the air, then so were ghosts.

The Geography of Christmas Specters

Today, Christmas and Hallowe'en tend to be very clearly distinguished and delineated by those who celebrate. The cozy holiday versus the spooky holiday; the one about family and nostalgia versus the one about horror and witchcraft. In the nineteenth century, these holidays were a little more nuanced than that, and their traditions and celebrations varied from region to region. In the United States, Hallowe'en became the designated day for frights and chills, but in England, where Hallowe'en was not celebrated as enthusiastically, Christmas was the season for ghost stories.[191]

As with most Victorian legends and folkloric beliefs, Christmas ghost stories were often rooted in a strong sense of place and community. One Victorian writer, who penned a piece on holiday ghosts for the *Liverpool Mercury* in 1894, described the regional character of seasonal legends:

....

191. Yuko, "How Ghost Stories Became a Christmas Tradition in Victorian England."

Norfolk and Suffolk, for instance, still have their legends of "white women" haunting particular spots, of coaches "drawn by horses without heads," and sometimes accompanied by spectral and headless grooms and outriders, of monstrous white dogs, footless ghosts, and uneasy spirits that refuse to be laid. Many other parts of the country are equally favoured with ghostly traditions; and when the villagers gathered within the squire's hospitable walls, as the ale circulated and the shadows in the hall deepened, stories of white witches and wise men, and tales of headless horsemen and phantom coaches, midnight monsters, and restless churchyard sprites, with many another tradition of legendary horror, would pass from lip to lip ...[192]

One intriguing Scottish legend, entirely new to me, was recorded by T. F. Thiselton-Dyer in *The Ghost World*, his compendium of spectral legends. Thiselton-Dyer refers to a folkloric belief that children born on Christmas would be capable of both seeing and even commanding spirits.[193] This seems like something that would have piqued the interest of the spiritualists, who were always curious which factors might predispose someone to mediumship or spirit communication, but I have not been able to find any evidence that they investigated or wrote about this belief.

Another haunting piece of Christmas lore, recorded in John Glyde's book of folklore, *The Norfolk Garland*, is as follows:

Many legends of bells under ground and under water are known in various parts of England. Where the churches are

....
192. "Christmas Ghosts," *Liverpool Mercury*, December 25, 1894.
193. Thiselton-Dyer, *The Ghost World*, 216.

said to have been swallowed up either by earthquake or the ravages of the sea, the old church bells are said to ring, deep, deep in the earth, every Christmas morning, and people go forth and put their ears to the ground, hoping to catch the music of the mysterious chimes in the subterranean temple.[194]

To me, this vision of phantom bells ringing out from the deep every year captures the spectral spirit of Victorian Christmastime.

The Origin of the Cozy Christmas

Across the nineteenth century, the Christmas holiday transformed dramatically, evolving from a date of only moderate importance into a major event and cultural phenomenon.[195] This metamorphosis of Christmas was part of a larger cultural shift driven by the Victorian middle class, which expanded significantly during the nineteenth century. Just as many of our ideas about what looks spooky, gothic, or haunted originate from the Victorian era, our modern sense of what's cozy, homey, and domestic is also colored by nineteenth-century sensibilities.

As Britain became more industrialized, people left the villages and hamlets of the countryside to seek economic opportunity in the city. This increased urbanization sparked the desire to cultivate a warm and sheltered environment in the family home so that people who felt battered by the daily grind of city life could at least return to a cozy and cheerful refuge at the end of the day. The growing middle class quickly developed an appetite for the material comforts of modern life, fueling Victorian consumerism. With factories popping up all over and increasing varieties of consumer goods available,

....

194. Glyde, *The Norfolk Garland*, 67.
195. Storey, "The Invention of the English Christmas," 17, 19–22.

there was booming demand for furnishings, décor, and toys. As the Victorian taste for domestic comforts grew, Christmas became more and more popular, and Christmas celebrations were increasingly lavish and elaborate.[196] Even ghost stories were caught up in the commercial Christmas boom, as books, especially books of ghost stories, became very popular Christmas gifts.[197]

Why Ghost Stories?

For generations, there had been a loose association between ghosts and midwinter in Britain, but as Christmas became a much more enthusiastically celebrated holiday with many more associated traditions, the old link between specters and Christmastime spawned a craze for holiday ghost stories. As the extravagance of the Victorian Christmas season increased, its ghostly traditions grew ever more powerful.[198] Thiselton-Dyer speculated that the Christmas season was particularly rife with ghost sightings because it was customary for the gentry to return to their ancestral family homes in the countryside during the Christmas holiday.[199] If the spirit of an ancestor had any messages or warnings to impart to younger generations, the Christmas season was one time when the entire family was assembled at the estate.

It makes sense that, for Victorians wealthy enough to have a city home and a country home (and for any companions or staff who traveled with them), leaving the bustle of the city and returning to the countryside each winter might feel like slipping backward in time. Half-forgotten memories could be refreshed, long-dead

....

196. Storey, "The Invention of the English Christmas," 20–22.
197. Cox and Gilbert, *The Oxford Book of Victorian Ghost Stories*, xii–xiv.
198. Briggs, "The Ghost Story," 180–81.
199. Thiselton-Dyer, *The Ghost World*, 382–83.

ancestors might feel much closer, family traditions could continue another year, and the years would begin to blur as swift and silent snow settled around the house. In the old manor, at once familiar and unfamiliar, all kinds of strange thoughts and memories might take root. So, what better way to spend one of the long winter nights than trading ghost stories around a fire?

It's a shame that many have abandoned the custom of telling ghost stories at Christmas. Though we now have a much more robust cultural celebration of Hallowe'en as the time of magic, mischief, and the macabre, there's something to be said for keeping a little of the edge, and some of the darker magic, in Christmas. At a time when many people are fixated on their shopping lists and their wish lists, what they've achieved in the past year and what they want in the coming year, it makes sense to insert a *memento mori*: a reminder that death comes for us all and you can't take your gifts with you. In fact, that is exactly the message of Charles Dickens's "A Christmas Carol" (1843), the most enduring and beloved classic Christmas ghost story. Dickens uses the four ghosts that visit his miserly protagonist, Ebenezer Scrooge, to remind the reader that no amount of worldly wealth is more important than kindness, compassion, and generosity. Arguably, our modern celebrations of Hallowe'en contain an element of this warning as well. People celebrate, decorate their homes and themselves, and eat delicious treats, but always with an edge, always with the reminder of death. Perhaps humans are just naturally drawn toward the marriage of revelry and death.

Spiritualists and the Ghosts of Christmas

Since spiritualists engaged in frequent spirit communication and often reported apparitions and spirit sightings, it's natural to wonder what they made of the Christmas ghost story tradition. I have not been able to find any evidence that serious spiritualists engaged in the same spooky storytelling that other Victorians enjoyed at Christmas. I suspect that for mediums, who considered a ghost sighting far more than just a scary story to share on a dark night, the tradition might have seemed too frivolous or irreverent. After all, for the spiritualists, an apparition was an important phenomenon worthy of being seriously recorded, reported, and studied. However, since many of the people who attended spirit circles were in mourning and sought connection with lost loved ones, it wouldn't be surprising if there was an uptick in séances around Christmas. Georgiana Houghton, one of the mediums discussed in more detail in chapter 4, definitely held plenty of sittings around the holidays, including on Christmas,[200] and New Year's Eve.[201] The spiritualists encouraged the bereaved to stay in touch with those who had passed beyond the veil, and the holidays are a time when people particularly long for connection with those they've lost.

Classic Victorian Ghost Stories

Here are just a few nineteenth-century ghost stories to give you a taste of the genre; the Elizabeth Gaskell story and both stories by Dickens were written and published specifically for the Christmas holiday, making them delightful seasonal reads.

+ "A Christmas Carol" and "The Signal-Man" by Charles Dickens
+ "The Old Nurse's Story" by Elizabeth Gaskell
+ "The Open Door" by Margaret Oliphant

....

200. Houghton, *Chronicles of the Photographs of Spiritual Beings and Phenomena Invisible to the Material Eye*, 100–102.
201. Houghton, *Evenings at Home in Spiritual Séance*, 284–85.

- "Ligeia" and "Morella" by Edgar Allan Poe
- "The Turn of the Screw" by Henry James

Try It Yourself

There are many benefits to exploring the shades and shadows that lurk in the final weeks of December. For those who are bereaved or who have painful memories connected to the holidays, honoring the darkness as well as the light at this time of the year might help with processing conflicted emotions. Meanwhile, even the most cheerful of holiday revelers might experience bittersweet nostalgia or poignant moments that highlight the inexorable passage of time. Around the holidays, the mandatory cheer that permeates the air can sometimes feel more oppressive than festive, so taking time to acknowledge the sorrowful as well as the sweet can be healthy and may enhance the experience of the holidays.

Tell Ghost Stories

Of all the Victorian traditions discussed in this book, spooky or spiritualist, the telling of holiday ghost stories might be the easiest one to revive. There are many ways to add the haunting and crystalline magic of a chilling ghost story to our modern celebrations (and you can add ghost stories to any holiday, not just Christmas). If you just want to introduce a shiver or two to your festivities, you can put a very modern spin on the practice by watching scary films, listening to eerie podcasts, or even staying up late reading terrifying anonymous internet stories. But if your aim is to recreate the tradition as authentically as possible, then you should have friends over for a holiday celebration and close the evening with a round of ghost stories.

For those who desire an authentically Victorian flavor, here's one tip for telling a ghost story like a Victorian: hit close to home.

Victorians liked to tell very personal ghost stories, rooted in specific people or places. Many guests, called upon to share a ghost story, might report something chilling or mysterious that they claimed to have experienced themselves. Others would share local legends from their hometown or frightening stories that had been passed down to them by family members. Lots of ghost stories centered on a particular location: a certain crossroads, an old bridge, or a nearby churchyard. So, think locally. Is there a particularly creepy abandoned house that you pass every day on your commute to work? Tell a harrowing tale about why it's abandoned.

Hold a Christmas (or Yule, or Solstice, or Hanukkah) Séance

For us, séances are so strongly associated with Hallowe'en that it can be odd to imagine Christmas as a prime time for spirit communication, but if you think about it, Christmas might be the ideal season for spirit circles. Christmas and other family-oriented annual celebrations have a way of pulling us backward in time, reminding us of holidays past and loved ones long gone. If you're in the Northern Hemisphere and Christmas falls in the middle of the winter for you, then there are additional reminders of death: trees without leaves, animals in hibernation, and familiar sights frosted over and ghostly in the long nights.

For those who have lost people close to them, the celebration of Christmas, Hanukkah, or any other holiday that is rooted in childhood, family, and cultural traditions might be extremely difficult. The sadness can be overwhelming and isolating as everyone else in the world seems to be heedlessly celebrating the season without the same grief. This is not a new sorrow; bereaved Victorians would have faced the same misery (though they did live in a culture that took mourning more seriously). Given that the holiday season can stir up melancholy, nostalgia, loneliness, and longing just as readily as joy and contentment, it makes sense that the desire for spirit communication might be at an all-time high around the Christmas season. So, following in the footsteps of Georgiana Houghton, hold a séance as one of your seasonal activities this year. If you celebrate a holiday other than Christmas, such as Yule or Hannukah, then you can tweak the suggestions below to make them fit your seasonal celebration. You can also just hold a séance on the solstice as a reflective practice, without connecting it to any established holiday.

Before you begin, you might spend some time setting up a space that pulls you back to another time or place. You can put old family photos on the kitchen table, add a few heirlooms or past Christmas gifts that remind you of your loved ones, and even prepare some holiday food or drink. Many spiritualists liked to open their séances by singing hymns; given that Christmas is a very musical holiday with so many associated tunes and lyrics, consider opening your Christmas séance with music. However you choose to open the séance, you can then follow the séance exercise from the first chapter in this book—using either the solitary or the group instructions depending on whether you're alone or with company.

Conclusion

The spiritualists described in these pages, devout, curious, dauntless, and inventive as they were, have all themselves passed into the *spirit-land*—the very place that they were fascinated by all their lives. They have moved on to find their answers and left their questions behind for us to ponder. Their ideas and practices live on—in modern Theosophy, spiritualism, and Western occultism but also in internet memes about spirit guides, in paranormal investigation shows, and in any number of séance scenes from books and films.

I like to think of this book as its own form of spirit communication, allowing these figures to walk alongside you and me, to share their practices, philosophies, and fears one more time. Some famous spiritualists were certainly less than sincere. Some saw mediumship as a financial opportunity rather than a spiritual one, but others were in earnest from their first séance until their last breath. Many existed in the ambiguous in-between, convinced by some supernatural phenomena while skeptical of others. All were shaped by the society in which they lived and died, but plenty were trying to be on the right side of history, to move the needle forward toward justice somehow.

Spiritualism was a movement formed on a tide of grief and loss, but it was also saturated with optimism and curiosity. Adherents saw themselves as living on the cusp of a new and more enlightened age, a time when all the answers would be revealed and all those lost would be restored to their loved ones. While our present time has proved to be quite different from the future that Victorian spiritualists and mystics imagined, their curiosity, relentless inventiveness, and defiant eccentricity are always available to us. They remind us to honor old wisdom while fighting for a new world, and they push us to be expansive and imaginative in our vision for the future. Their spirit endures not just in nineteenth-century archives and museum exhibits but in every teenager experimenting with their first deck of tarot cards.

Glossary

automatism: The practice of creating art or writing "automatically" or "unconsciously"—usually in hopes of receiving a channeled message or revelation from one's own unconscious.

ghost-seers: People with a particular predilection for seeing spirits invisible to others. The idea of ghost-seers predates séances, spiritualism, and the advent of professional spiritualist mediums in the nineteenth century.

medievalism: The Victorian reverence for early British history, folklore, and legend. Victorian Medievalism was reflected in lots of nineteenth-century art, from Pre-Raphaelite paintings to Tennyson's Arthurian poetry.

mesmerism: Also called "animal magnetism," mesmerism was a practice developed by Dr. Franz Mesmer, who believed that it was a potent healing tool. During mesmerism, the doctor, or mesmerist, would put their patient into a trance and then try to "unblock" and restore the natural current of an invisible magnetic fluid that was believed to flow throw all human bodies.

phenomena: Strange sights, sounds, or sensations that appear to indicate supernatural activity. Phenomena were very important to spiritualists and paranormal investigators, who sought to study and categorize them.

spirit guide: A term used by mediums to describe spirits who they believed acted in a benevolent or guiding capacity. They were also called "spirit controls" because they were believed to be capable of controlling the medium's voice and/or body to channel communications through them.

spirit-land: The place where spirits congregated and could be communicated with. Also known as the borderland.

Theosophy: A religion that began with the founding of the occultist Theosophical Society in 1875. Like spiritualists, Theosophists were interested in categorizing supernatural phenomena, but they prioritized the study of occult mysteries over spirit communication and trance performance.

thought transference: Another name for telepathy.

Recommended Reading

Halloween: Romantic Art and Customs of Yesteryear by Diane Arkins

The Other World: Spiritualism and Psychical Research in England, 1850–1914 by Janet Oppenheim

Radical Spirits: Spiritualism and Women's Rights in Nineteenth-Century America by Ann Braude

Strange and Secret Peoples: Fairies and Victorian Consciousness by Carole G. Silver

Victorian Ghosts in the Noontide: Women Writers and the Supernatural by Vanessa D. Dickerson

Victorian Women and the Theatre of Trance: Mediums, Spiritualists, and Mesmerists in Performance by Amy Lehman

Bibliography

Alexander, Michael. *Medievalism: The Middle Ages in Modern England*. New Haven, CT: Yale University Press, 2017.

Aptowicz, Cristin O'Keefe. *Dr. Mütter's Marvels: A True Tale of Intrigue and Innovation at the Dawn of Modern Medicine*. New York: Avery, 2014.

Arkins, Diane C. *Halloween: Romantic Art and Customs of Yesteryear*. Gretna, LA: Pelican Publishing, 2000.

Arntfield, Michael. *Gothic Forensics: Criminal Investigative Procedure in Victorian Horror & Mystery*. New York: Palgrave Macmillan, 2016.

"The Art of Crystal-Gazing." *Borderland* 1, no. 2 (October 1893): 117–127.

"Automatic Handwriting." *Borderland* 1, no. 4 (April 1894): 340–341.

"Auto-Telepathic Writing." *Borderland* 1, no. 1 (July 1893): 50–51.

Bell, Michael J. "William Wells Newell and the Foundation of American Folklore Scholarship." *Journal of the Folklore Institute* 10, no. 1/2 (June–August 1973): 7–21.

Braid, James. *Neurypnology; or, the Rationale of Nervous Sleep, Considered in Relation with Animal Magnetism.* London: John Churchill, 1843.

Braude, Ann. *Radical Spirits: Spiritualism and Women's Rights in Nineteenth-Century America.* 2nd ed. Bloomington, IN: Indiana University Press, 2001.

Briggs, Julia. "The Ghost Story." In *A New Companion to the Gothic,* edited by David Punter, 176–185. Oxford: Blackwell Publishing, 2012.

Buchanan, Joseph Rodes. *Manual of Psychometry: The Dawn of a New Civilization.* Boston: Joseph Rodes Buchanan, 1885.

Burnett, Charles S. F. "The Earliest Chiromancy in the West." *Journal of the Warburg and Courtauld Institutes* 50, no. 1 (1987): 189–195.

"The Case of Mary Stannard." *The Woman's Journal,* October 26, 1878. *British Library Newspapers.* Accessed December 26, 2022.

"Character Reading by Palmistry and Otherwise." *Borderland* 2, no. 1 (January 1895): 60–65.

"Christmas Ghosts." *Liverpool Mercury,* December 25, 1894. *British Library Newspapers.* Accessed December 10, 2022.

"The Chronique of the Quarter." *Borderland* 1, no. 5 (July 1894): 399–401.

Cook, Susan E. "Hidden Mothers: Forms of Absence in Victorian Photography and Fiction." *Nineteenth-Century Gender Studies* 17, no. 3 (Winter 2021).

Cox, Michael, and R. A. Gilbert. Introduction to *The Oxford Book of Victorian Ghost Stories*. Oxford: Oxford University Press, 1991.

Crowe, Catherine. *The Night-Side of Nature; or, Ghosts and Ghost Seers*. 1847. Reprint, London: George Routledge and Sons, 1866.

"The Cruelty of Superstition." *Borderland* 2, no. 2 (April 1895): 137–138.

Denton, William, and Elizabeth M. F. Denton. *The Soul of Things; or, Psychometric Researches and Discoveries*. Boston: Walker, Wise and Company, 1863.

Dickerson, Vanessa D. *Victorian Ghosts in the Noontide: Women Writers and the Supernatural*. Columbia, MO: University of Missouri Press, 1996.

Doyle, Arthur Conan. *The Coming of the Fairies*. London: Hodder and Stoughton, 1922.

———. *The History of Spiritualism*. 2 vols. London: Cassell, 1926.

Ellis, R. J., and Henry Louis Gates Jr. "'Grievances at the treatment she received': Harriet E. Wilson's Spiritualist Career in Boston, 1868–1900." *American Literary History* 24, no. 2 (Summer 2012): 234–264.

"Extraordinary Revelations from the Other World." *Daily Gazette for Middlesbrough*, October 6, 1888. *British Library Newspapers*. Accessed December 26, 2022.

"Friday's and Saturday's Posts." *Hampshire Chronicle*, January 9, 1804. *British Library Newspapers*. Accessed January 21, 2023.

Forsberg, Laura. "Nature's Invisibilia: The Victorian Microscope and the Miniature Fairy." *Victorian Studies* 57, no. 4 (Summer 2015): 638–666.

"Getting a Spirit Photograph." *Wild Oats*, October 29, 1874. *British Library Newspapers*. Accessed December 26, 2023.

"Ghost Hunting in Durham." York Herald, September 24, 1892. British Library Newspapers. Accessed December 10, 2022.

Greenaway, Kate. *Language of Flowers*. London: George Routledge and Sons, 1884.

Greenblatt, Stephen, and M. H. Abrams, eds. *The Norton Anthology of English Literature*. Vol. 2, 9th ed. New York: W.W. Norton, 2012.

Glyde, John. *The Norfolk Garland: A Collection of the Superstitious Beliefs and Practices, Proverbs, Curious Customs, Ballads, and Songs, of the People of Norfolk, as well as Anecdotes Illustrative of the Genius or Peculiarities of Norfolk Celebrities*. London: Jarrold & Sons, 1872.

"For Halloween." *Good Housekeeping*, October 1904. *Women's Magazine Archive*. Accessed January 2, 2023.

"Hallowe'en or Harvest Dishes." *Ladies' Home Journal*, November 1900. *Women's Magazine Archive*. Accessed January 2, 2023.

"The Hammersmith Ghost!" *Hull Packet*, January 17, 1804. *British Library Newspapers*. Accessed January 21, 2023.

Hammond, D. Corydon. "A Review of the History of Hypnosis through the Late 19th Century." *American Journal of Clinical Hypnosis* 56, no. 2 (October 2013): 174–191.

Hardinge, Emma. *Rules to Be Observed When Forming Spiritual Circles*. Boston: Colby and Rich, 1887.

Harper, Margaret Mills. *Wisdom of Two: The Spiritual and Literary Collaboration of George and W. B. Yeats*. Oxford: Oxford University Press, 2006.

Houghton, Georgiana. *Chronicles of the Photographs of Spiritual Beings and Phenomena Invisible to the Material Eye: Interblended with Personal Narrative*. London: E. W. Allen, 1882.

————. *Evenings at Home in Spiritual Séance: Welded Together by a Species of Autobiography*. London: E. W. Allen, 1882.

Hutton, Ronald. "Witches and Cunning Folk in British Literature 1800–1940." *Preternature: Critical and Historical Studies on the Preternatural* 7, no. 1 (2018): 27–49.

Ingram, M. V. *An Authenticated History of the Famous Bell Witch*. Nashville: Setliff, 1894.

Jacobs, Steven. *Framing Pictures: Film and the Visual Arts*. Edinburgh: Edinburgh University Press, 2011.

Johnston, Theresa. "Mrs. Stanford and the Netherworld." *Stanford Magazine*, May/June 2000.

"A Jolly Hallowe'en Party." *Ladies' Home Journal*, October 1902. *Women's Magazine Archive*. Accessed January 2, 2023.

Keightley, Thomas. *The Fairy Mythology: Illustrative of the Romance and Superstition of Various Countries*. 1828. Reprint, London: George Bell & Sons, 1892.

Kelley, Ruth Edna. *The Book of Hallowe'en*. Boston: Lothrop, Lee & Shepard, 1919.

Lawford, Louisa. *The Fortune-Teller; or, Peeps into Futurity*. London: Routledge, Warne, and Routledge, 1861.

Lehman, Amy. *Victorian Women and the Theatre of Trance: Mediums, Spiritualists, and Mesmerists in Performance*. Jefferson, NC: McFarland, 2009.

Lepine, Ayla. "The Pre-Raphaelites: Medievalism and Victorian Visual Culture." In *The Oxford Handbook of Victorian Medievalism*, edited by Joanne Parker and Corinna Wagner, 488–506. Oxford: Oxford University Press, 2020.

Levine, Naomi. "Tirra-Lirrical Ballads: Source Hunting with the Lady of Shalott." *Victorian Poetry* 54, no. 4 (Winter 2016): 439–454.

Linkman, Audrey. "Taken from Life: Post-Mortem Portraiture in Britain 1860–1910." *History of Photography* 30, no. 4 (Winter 2006): 309–347.

Mackley, J. S. "Spring-Heeled Jack: The Terror of London." *Aeternum: The Journal of Contemporary Gothic Studies* 3, no. 2 (December 2016): 1–20.

"Magnetic Healing." *Banner of Light* 87, no. 16 (June 16, 1900): 5.

"Magnetic Healing!" *Emporia Gazette*, April 20, 1899. Nineteenth Century U.S. Newspapers. Accessed December 10, 2022.

Manseau, Peter. *The Apparitionists: A Tale of Phantoms, Fraud, Photography, and the Man Who Captured Lincoln's Ghost*. Boston: Houghton Mifflin Harcourt, 2017.

McCrary, Charles. "Fortune Telling and American Religious Freedom." *Religion and American Culture: A Journal of Interpretation* 28, no. 2 (Summer 2018): 269–306.

"Miscellaneous." *The Boston Investigator*, June 2, 1880. *British Library Newspapers*. Accessed December 26, 2022.

Montgomery, Horace. "Resurrection Times." *The Georgia Review* 43, no. 3 (Fall 1989): 531–544.

Moore, Kate. "Declared Insane for Speaking Up: The Dark American History of Silencing Women through Psychiatry." *Time*, June 22, 2021. https://time.com/6074783/psychiatry-history-women-mental-health/.

"More about Crystal-Gazing," *Borderland* 1, no. 6 (October 1894): 529–530.

"More about Automatic Writing." *Borderland* 1, no. 2 (October 1893): 166–169.

"My Experience in Automatic Writing." *Borderland* 1, no. 1 (July 1893): 39–49.

Navarre, Joan. "Oscar Wilde, Edward Heron-Allen, and the Palmistry Craze of the 1880s." *English Literature in Transition, 1880–1920* 54, No. 2 (2011): 174–184.

"Old and New for Halloween: How Individual Fortunes Are Divined by the Fates." *Good Housekeeping*, October 1892. *Women's Magazine Archive*. Accessed January 2, 2023.

Oppenheim, Janet. *The Other World: Spiritualism and Psychical Research in England, 1850–1914*. Cambridge: Cambridge University Press, 1985.

Perkins, Maureen. *The Reform of Time: Magic and Modernity*. London: Pluto Press, 2001.

"Prosecution of a Palmist." *Borderland* 1, no. 2 (October 1893): 185.

"Result of the Test Experiment in Reading Unknown Hands." *Borderland* 1, no. 2 (October 1893): 179–184.

Robinson, Michael. *The Pre-Raphaelites: Their Lives and Works in 500 Images.* London: Lorenz Books, 2020.

Schlager, Patricius. "Gervase of Tilbury." In the *Catholic Encyclopedia*, vol. 6, edited by Charles George Herbermann, Edward A. Pace, Condé B. Pallen, Thomas J. Shahan, and John J. Wynne, 536. New York: Robert Appleton Company, 1909.

"Seeking Counsel of the Wise." *Borderland* 1, no. 1 (July 1893): 7–9.

Seeman, Erik R. *Speaking with the Dead in Early America.* Philadelphia: University of Pennsylvania Press, 2019.

"Servant Girls and Fortune Tellers." *Manchester Courier and Lancashire General Advertiser*, May 1, 1886. *British Library Newspapers.* Accessed December 10, 2022.

Silver, Carole G. *Strange and Secret Peoples: Fairies and Victorian Consciousness.* New York: Oxford University Press, 1999.

Simpson, Jacqueline, and Steve Roud. *A Dictionary of English Folklore.* Oxford: Oxford University Press, 2000.

Sims, Michael, ed. *The Penguin Book of Victorian Women in Crime: Forgotten Cops and Private Eyes from the Time of Sherlock Holmes.* New York: Penguin Books, 2011.

Smith, Elise Lawton. "The Art of Evelyn De Morgan." *Woman's Art Journal* 18, no. 2 (Autumn 1997–Winter 1998): 3–10.

"Spirit Photography: Progress in Photographing Invisibles." *Borderland* 1, no. 5 (July 1894): 443–446.

Bibliography

Stoker, Bram. *Dracula*. New York: Penguin, 2003.

Storey, John. "The Invention of the English Christmas." In *Christmas, Ideology and Popular Culture*, edited by Sheila Whiteley, 17–31. Edinburgh: Edinburgh University Press, 2008.

"The Study of Palmistry." *Borderland* 1, no. 1 (July 1893): 75–77.

"The Study of Psychical Phenomena: A Historical Summary." *Borderland* 1, no. 1 (July 1893): 24–26.

"Superstitions of Hallow-e'en." *Ladies' Home Journal*, October 1892. *Women's Magazine Archive*. Accessed January 2, 2023.

Taylor, J. Traill, H. R. Haweis, and James Robertson. *The Veil Lifted: Modern Developments of Spirit Photography*. Edited by Andrew Glendinning. London: Whittaker, 1894.

Tennyson, Alfred Lord. *Poems*. London: Edward Moxon, 1833.

Thiselton-Dyer, T. F., *The Ghost World*. London: Ward & Downey, 1893.

Yeats, W. B. *The Poetical Works of William B. Yeats*. 2 Vols. New York: Macmillan, 1906.

Yuko, Elizabeth. "How Ghost Stories Became a Christmas Tradition in Victorian England." History.com. December 15, 2021. https://www.history.com/news/christmas-tradition-ghost-stories.

Notes

Notes

Notes

To Write to the Author

If you wish to contact the author or would like more information about this book, please write to the author in care of Llewellyn Worldwide Ltd. and we will forward your request. Both the author and the publisher appreciate hearing from you and learning of your enjoyment of this book and how it has helped you. Llewellyn Worldwide Ltd. cannot guarantee that every letter written to the author can be answered, but all will be forwarded. Please write to:

Steele Alexandra Douris
℅ Llewellyn Worldwide
2143 Wooddale Drive
Woodbury, MN 55125-2989
Please enclose a self-addressed stamped envelope for reply,
or $1.00 to cover costs. If outside the U.S.A., enclose
an international postal reply coupon.

Many of Llewellyn's authors have websites with additional information and resources. For more information, please visit our website at http://www.llewellyn.com.